Demographic and Family Transition in Southeast Asia

Wei-Jun Jean Yeung

Demographic and Family Transition in Southeast Asia

Wei-Jun Jean Yeung
Department of Sociology
National University of Singapore
Singapore, Singapore

ISBN 978-3-030-85678-6   ISBN 978-3-030-85679-3 (eBook)
https://doi.org/10.1007/978-3-030-85679-3

© The Editor(s) (if applicable) and The Author(s) 2022. This book is an open access publication.
Open Access This book is licensed under the terms of the Creative Commons Attribution 4.0 International License (http://creativecommons.org/licenses/by/4.0/), which permits use, sharing, adaptation, distribution and reproduction in any medium or format, as long as you give appropriate credit to the original author(s) and the source, provide a link to the Creative Commons license and indicate if changes were made.

The images or other third party material in this book are included in the book's Creative Commons license, unless indicated otherwise in a credit line to the material. If material is not included in the book's Creative Commons license and your intended use is not permitted by statutory regulation or exceeds the permitted use, you will need to obtain permission directly from the copyright holder.

The use of general descriptive names, registered names, trademarks, service marks, etc. in this publication does not imply, even in the absence of a specific statement, that such names are exempt from the relevant protective laws and regulations and therefore free for general use.

The publisher, the authors and the editors are safe to assume that the advice and information in this book are believed to be true and accurate at the date of publication. Neither the publisher nor the authors or the editors give a warranty, expressed or implied, with respect to the material contained herein or for any errors or omissions that may have been made. The publisher remains neutral with regard to jurisdictional claims in published maps and institutional affiliations.

This Springer imprint is published by the registered company Springer Nature Switzerland AG
The registered company address is: Gewerbestrasse 11, 6330 Cham, Switzerland

Preface

Southeast Asia is one of the most diverse regions in the world, hosting four major religions, hundreds of languages, innumerable ethnicities, and radically diverging political systems and cultures. The Southeast Asian countries are important because they are large in aggregate, strategically located, exceptionally diverse, and intellectually interesting. The region's economic and geopolitical profile in the world has risen dramatically over the past decade. In global international relations, the increasingly integrated Association of Southeast Asian Nations (ASEAN) has become the hub of the emerging regional security architecture of the Asia-Pacific. Founded in 1967, ASEAN today encompasses Brunei, Cambodia, Indonesia, Laos, Malaysia, Myanmar, the Philippines, Singapore, Thailand, and Vietnam—economies at vastly different stages of development but all with immense growth potential. Timor-Leste is the only Southeast Asian country that is not a part of ASEAN now although it has engaged closely economically with ASEAN countries. The region is at the centre of a profound transformation in Asia-Pacific.

Currently, Southeast Asia is one of the fastest growing markets though one of the least well known. The region is a major global hub of manufacturing and trade, and one of the fastest-growing consumer markets in the world. Southeast Asia's sea lanes have more than half of the world's merchant tonnage and one-third of global maritime traffic transiting the region every day from the Persian Gulf and the Indian Ocean to Northeast Asian countries such as China, Japan, and Korea.

As Southeast Asia's economic and geopolitical importance sets to expand in the next decade, it is crucial for those outside the region to understand its complexities and contradictions. It is the objective of this book to introduce Southeast Asia to more readers. As one of the most diverse regions in the world, it is hazardous to view Southeast Asia as one homogeneous block. For example, Singapore's GDP per capita is more than 50 times higher than that in Cambodia, Myanmar, and Timor-Leste. In terms of culture and religion, Indonesia, for example, is almost 90 percent Muslim, while the Philippines is more than 80 percent Roman Catholic, Thailand is more than 95 percent Buddhist, and Singapore has multiple religious and ethnic groups.

This book aims to document the history of demographic and family transitions in the last half a century that contextualized the socio-economic changes in Southeast

Asia and to help readers anticipate future development in this region. Demographic behaviours such as marriage and childbirth shape the population size and structure of a country that determine how large and young (or old) a population is now and in the future. As the family is the most basic social and economic unit in the society, it is important to understand how this institution has been changing over time in this region. The education and health of the youth and children are the most valuable human capital of a country that affects the future development of the region. Data presented here are limited to the availability of time-series data for the countries. Notably, migration patterns and people's attitudes are missing in this book because comparable data for all countries over time are lacking.

The book is meant to be a resource book with data from many different sources collated for easy reference. The process of assembling these data took several years. Credits go to Ms. Lori Jane Pasaraba and Ms. Nawal Binti Mohamed Hashim, who were Research Associate and Research Assistant at the Centre for Family and Population Research (CFPR) at the National University of Singapore at the time of this manuscript's preparation, for helping to collect data, review literature, prepare graphs, and edit this book. The generous support from the Stephen Riady Foundation, OUE Limited, and Lippo Group is gratefully acknowledged. Without their support, this book would not have been possible to complete. Thanks also go to the helpful comments of two anonymous reviewers on an earlier draft of this book. We hope this book will become a handy resource for scholars, practitioners, and the general public who are interested in Southeast Asia.

Singapore, Singapore Wei-Jun Jean Yeung

Contents

Part I Population, Marriage, Fertility and Household Structures

1 Introduction 3
   1.1 Background for Family Transition in Southeast Asia 5
   1.2 Explaining Global Family Changes 5
       1.2.1 Historical Context 6
       1.2.2 Kinship Patterns 7
       1.2.3 Cultural Diversity 7
   1.3 Changes in Southeast Asian Families 8
       1.3.1 Changing Marriage Patterns 8
       1.3.2 Fertility Trends 8
       1.3.3 Living Arrangements 8
   1.4 Socio-economic Contexts and Transformation 9
   1.5 Highlights of the Trends and Patterns 10
       1.5.1 Population 10
       1.5.2 Socio-economic Development 11
       1.5.3 Union Formation and Dissolution 11
       1.5.4 Childbearing 12
       1.5.5 Household Structure 12
       1.5.6 Education 13
       1.5.7 Youth Unemployment 13
       1.5.8 Child Health 14
   References 14

2 Trends in Population and Socioeconomic Development in Southeast Asia 17
   2.1 Population Structure of Southeast Asia 17
   2.2 Population Density 22
   2.3 Level of Economic Development 24
   2.4 Education 26
   2.5 Female Labour Force Participation 28
   2.6 Gender Inequality Index (GII) 29

		References	30
3	**Marriage**		33
	3.1	Singulate Mean Age at Marriage (SMAM)	33
	3.2	Singlehood	35
	3.3	Divorce	39
	3.4	Consensual Union	40
		References	42
4	**Fertility**		45
	4.1	Total Fertility Rate (TFR)	45
	4.2	Mean Age at Childbearing (MAC)	47
	4.3	Age-Specific Fertility Rates (ASFR)	49
	4.4	Adolescent Fertility Rates	53
	4.5	Childlessness	54
	4.6	Ideal and Actual Fertility Rates	58
		References	59
5	**Household Structures**		61
	5.1	Average Household Size in Southeast Asia, 1980–2010	61
	5.2	Household Types in Southeast Asia, 1970–2010	62
		5.2.1 Nuclear Households with Children	62
		5.2.2 Number of Nuclear Households Without Children Are Rising	63
		5.2.3 No Clear Trend for Extended Family Households	64
		5.2.4 Decreasing Single-Parent Households	65
		5.2.5 Drop in the Prevalence of Composite Households	66
		5.2.6 Rising One-Person Households	67
	5.3	Living Arrangements Among Older Adults in Southeast Asia	68
		5.3.1 Living with Their Children or Spouse	69
		5.3.2 Rise in the Number of Independently Living Older Adults	70
		References	73

Part II Child and Youth Well-Being

6	**Education and Youth Unemployment in Southeast Asia**		77
	6.1	Youth Literacy Rates	77
	6.2	Expected Years in Full-Time Education	78
	6.3	Rate of Out-Of-School Children of Primary School Age	80
	6.4	Transition Rate from Primary to Lower Secondary Education	81
	6.5	Gross Secondary Enrolment Ratio	83
	6.6	Gender Parity Index (GPI) in Southeast Asia	84
		6.6.1 GPI for Primary School Enrolment	84
		6.6.2 GPI for Secondary School Enrolment	86
		6.6.3 GPI for Tertiary School Enrolment	87

	6.7	Gender Differences in University Graduates by Fields of Study	88
	6.8	Population with at least Completed Upper Secondary Education	90
	6.9	Population with at least Completed Tertiary Education	92
	6.10	Youth Unemployment in Southeast Asia	93
	References		96
7	**Child Health in Southeast Asia**		99
	7.1	Low-Birthweight Babies	99
	7.2	Prevalence of Overweight (% of Children Under 5)	101
	7.3	Prevalence of Wasting (% of Children Under 5)	103
	7.4	Exclusive Breastfeeding Rate	105
	References		106
8	**Conclusion**		109
	Reference		112

List of Figures

Fig. 2.1	Total population of Southeast Asian countries, 1960–2015	18
Fig. 2.2	Percentage of total population aged 65 and above in Southeast Asia, 1960–2015	18
Fig. 2.3	Old-age dependency ratio in Southeast Asia, 1950–2015	20
Fig. 2.4	Child dependency ratio in Southeast Asia, 1950–2015	20
Fig. 2.5	Proportion of oldest old in Southeast Asia, 1950–2015	21
Fig. 2.6	Life expectancy at birth in Southeast Asia, 1960–2015	22
Fig. 2.7	**a** Population density of Southeast Asian countries, 1960–2015, **b** population density of Southeast Asian countries excluding Singapore, 1960–2015	23
Fig. 2.8	**a** GDP per capita of Southeast Asian countries, 1990–2015, **b** GDP per capita of Southeast Asian countries excluding Singapore, Brunei, Malaysia and Thailand, 1990–2015	25
Fig. 2.9	Poverty headcount ratio of Southeast Asian countries at national poverty lines, 1995–2015	26
Fig. 2.10	**a** Gross tertiary enrolment ratio in Southeast Asia for both sexes, 1970–2015, **b** gross tertiary enrolment ratio for females in Southeast Asia, 1970–2015	27
Fig. 2.11	Female labour force participation rate in Southeast Asia, 1990–2015	29
Fig. 2.12	Gender Inequality Index (GII) in Southeast Asia, 1990–2015	30
Fig. 3.1	**a** SMAM for females in Southeast Asia, around 1970–2010, **b** SMAM for males in Southeast Asia, around 1970–2010	34
Fig. 3.2	**a** Singlehood rate among female 30–34-year-olds in Southeast Asia, 1980–2010, **b** singlehood rate among female 35–39-year-olds in Southeast Asia, 1980–2010	36

Fig. 3.3	**a** Singlehood rate among male 30–34-year-olds in Southeast Asia, 1980–2010, **b** singlehood rate among male 35–39-year-olds in Southeast Asia, 1980–2010	37
Fig. 3.4	Crude divorce rate in Southeast Asia, 1970–2015	39
Fig. 3.5	**a** Proportion of women in consensual unions in Southeast Asia, by country and age group, latest available year	41
Fig. 4.1	**a** TFR of low-fertility countries in Souheast Asia, 2014, **b** TFR of high-fertility countries in Southeast Asia, 2014	46
Fig. 4.2	**a** SEA countries with increasing, or little change in, MAC (as of 2010–2015), **b** SEA countries with decreasing MAC (as of 2010–2015)	48
Fig. 4.3	**a** ASFRs in high-fertility countries (as of 2010–2015), by age group, **b** ASFRs in low-fertility countries (as of 2010–2015), by age group	50
Fig. 4.4	Age-specific fertility rates in 1970–1975, 1990–1995, and 2010–2015	51
Fig. 4.5	Adolescent fertility rates (births per 1000 women aged 15–19) in Southeast Asia, 1960–2015	53
Fig. 4.6	Childlessness among women aged 40–44, years 2000, 2010	55
Fig. 4.7	Definitive childlessness among women in Southeast Asia aged 45–49 (2000, 2010)	56
Fig. 4.8	**a** Childless women per birth cohort, recorded in 2000. **b** Childless women per cohort in 2010	57
Fig. 4.9	Ideal and actual fertility rates, 2000, 2014	58
Fig. 5.1	Average household size in Southeast Asia, 1980–2010	62
Fig. 5.2	Percent of nuclear households with children in Southeast Asian countries, 1970–2010	63
Fig. 5.3	% of childless nuclear households in Southeast Asia, 1970–2010	64
Fig. 5.4	% of extended family households in Southeast Asia, 1970–2010	65
Fig. 5.5	% of single-parent households (SPH) in Southeast Asia, 1970–2010	66
Fig. 5.6	% of composite households in Southeast Asia, 1970–2010	67
Fig. 5.7	% of one-person households (OPH) in Southeast Asia, 1970–2010	68
Fig. 5.8	**a** % of elderly females living with at least one child in Southeast Asia, by latest available year, **b** % of elderly males living with at least one child in Southeast Asia, by latest available year	69

Fig. 5.9	**a** % of elderly females living solely with spouse in Southeast Asia, by latest available year, **b** % of elderly males living solely with spouse in Southeast Asia, by latest year	71
Fig. 5.10	**a** % of female elderly living alone in Southeast Asia, latest available year, **b** % of male elderly living alone in Southeast Asia, latest available year	72
Fig. 6.1	Literacy rates of 15–24-year-olds in Southeast Asia, 1990–2012	78
Fig. 6.2	Expected years in full-time education in Southeast Asia, 1980–2013	79
Fig. 6.3	Rate of out-of-school children of primary school age, 1970–2014	80
Fig. 6.4	Effective transition rate from primary to lower secondary general education in Southeast Asia, 1971–2014	82
Fig. 6.5	Gross secondary enrolment ratio in Southeast Asia for both sexes, 1970–2015	83
Fig. 6.6	Gender parity index for primary-level enrolment of Southeast Asia, 1990–2013	85
Fig. 6.7	Gender parity index for secondary-level enrolment of Southeast Asia, 1990–2013	86
Fig. 6.8	Gender parity index for tertiary-level enrolment of Southeast Asia, 1990–2013	88
Fig. 6.9	Percentage of female tertiary graduates in different fields of study in Southeast Asia, 1999–2015	89
Fig. 6.10	Percentage of population age 25+ with at least completed upper secondary education in Southeast Asia, 2000–2014	91
Fig. 6.11	Percentage of population age 25+ with at least completed tertiary education in Southeast Asia, 2000–2014	92
Fig. 6.12a	Youth (aged 15–24) unemployment rates in Southeast Asia, 1990–2015 (% of total labour force)	94
Fig. 6.12b	Female youth (aged 15–24) unemployment rates in Southeast Asia, 1990–2015 (% of total labour force)	94
Fig. 6.12c	Male youth (aged 15–24) unemployment rates in Southeast Asia, 1990–2015 (% of total labour force)	95
Fig. 7.1	Low-birthweight babies (% of births) of Southeast Asian countries, 1990–2015	100
Fig. 7.2	Prevalence of overweight (% of children under 5) of Southeast Asian countires, 1974–2015	102
Fig. 7.3	**a** Prevalence of wasting (% of children under 5), 1970–2015, **b** prevalence of severe wasting, weight for height (% of children under 5), 1970–2015	104
Fig. 7.4	Exclusive breastfeeding (% of children under 6 months) of Southeast Asian countries, 1995–2015	105

Part I
Population, Marriage, Fertility and Household Structures

Chapter 1
Introduction

In the past decade, Southeast Asia's economic and geopolitical profile in the world has risen dramatically. It is one of the fastest growing markets and least well-known regions in the world. Countries in this region are important because they are large in aggregate, strategically located, exceptionally diverse, and intellectually interesting. This book on Demographic and Family Changes in Southeast Asia (SEA) presents the trends and patterns of family changes from all eleven countries in the region for the past 50 years (till 2015). It collects indicators on marriage, fertility, and household structures, and child and youth well-being based on data that are dispersed in many different sources and compiles them in one single document making it easier for researchers, practitioners, and policy-makers who are interested in this diverse and rapidly growing region to refer to. The report is meant to be a resource book to provide a snapshot of changes in the last half a century in key demographic, socio-economic characteristics, and family structure in the region to facilitate an understanding of the transitions that have undergone. These trends and patterns are meant to help readers understand the levels of development and diversity in this region that can shape the future socioeconomic development in this region in the next few decades. The large amount of data presented here precludes in-depth interpretations due to space constraints. References are provided throughout this brief on various topics for readers who are interested in learning greater details to consult with.

A review of the literature on the structure of families in the region shows that contemporary studies on Southeast Asia focus on a handful of themes that focus on individual countries. In the marriage literature, for example, regional studies are done by a few scholars and commonly include Indonesia, Malaysia, the Philippines, Thailand, or Singapore, with the recent inclusion of Myanmar (Dommaraju & Jones, 2011; Jones, 1997, 2012; Jones & Shen, 2008; Jones & Yeung, 2014; Yeung & Hu, 2018). Brunei, Cambodia, Lao PDR, and Timor-Leste are frequently left out when scholars discuss Southeast Asia. While we acknowledge that issues of data availability in these countries play a big role in their absence in comparative studies, we stress that leaving them out may cause one to miss vital information on Southeast

Asia as a whole. Therefore, providing a comprehensive time trend of a set of indicators for all countries within the region is one of the objectives of this book.

In choosing which indicators to include, we drew heavily on major references such as the World Family Map prepared by the Child Trends and Social Trends Institute, and the Organisation for Economic Co-operation and Development (OECD) database indicators. Data used in the figures in this report are sourced from publicly available databases and reports such as the United Nations (UN) Data, Integrated Public Use Microdata Series (IPUMS) International Version 6.4, Association of Southeast Asian Nations (ASEAN) Statistics, World Bank Data, and various countries' statistical offices.

Such indicators were commonly used in the literature focusing on family and population changes. The choice of indicators to include in this report is mainly based on the availability of comparable data in the past four to five decades that allows a description of time trends. When data are available, a longer time series is presented. Some indicators have longer time series or gave more countries included than others due to the comparability and availability of the data.

This report is structured into two parts. Part A presents changes in demographic and household structures, and Part B presents changes in child and youth well-being. I begin with a brief introduction of the historical and cultural background of Southeast Asia that are crucial for understanding changes in Southeast Asia followed by a briefing on changes in population and socio-economic indicators in the past few decades to help users contextualize the statistics presented here. Subsequently, sections on detailed changes in marriage, fertility, and family structure were presented. The section on marriage includes indicators such as changes in marriage rates, age at marriage, the incidence of singlehood, and divorce. Alternative forms of partnership such as consensual unions or cohabitations which are used interchangeably in this report are also described. The section on fertility trends shows changes in fertility rates (total, age-specific, adolescent) and age at childbearing. Figures on ideal and actual fertility rates and childlessness rates in Southeast Asian countries are also included.

Chapter 5 presents information on trends in household structures in the region by examining changes in household sizes, and incidence of one-person households, single-parent families, as well as extended and composite households. Changes in the living arrangements of the elderly are also discussed.

Part 2 shows changes in child and youth well-being in the region including changes in education level, school enrolment, rate of out-of-school children, and gender parity index of education (Chap. 6), youth unemployment (Chap. 6), and child health which includes the prevalence of low-birthweight babies, overweight and wasting of children under 5, and breastfeeding rates (Chap. 7).

1.1 Background for Family Transition in Southeast Asia

Southeast South Asia is home to 8.5% of the world's population, including the world's fourth most populous countries—Indonesia and 10 other countries—Brunei, Malaysia, Philippines, Thailand, Vietnam, Cambodia, Laos, Myanmar, Singapore, and Timor-Leste. Countries in this region have undergone uneven development in the past half a century, providing a unique perspective on the intersection of culture, industrialization, public policies, and globalization in shaping the meaning and functioning of the family system around the world. The evolution of families in Southeast Asia is distinct from that in the neighbouring region of East Asia, where many of the family changes such as fertility and marriage trends have overshot those in Europe and North America in terms of the low fertility and marriage rate (Jones & Yeung, 2014; Raymo et al., 2015; Yeung et al., 2018).

While the fertility rate in East Asia was already below or near replacement level in 1990 and is now at ultra-low levels, it remains above replacement level in most countries in Southeast Asia, with total fertility rates (TFRs) above 2 in most countries and above 3 in several. Moreover, while mean age at marriage has risen in East Asia, with more than one-third of adults remaining single at age 40, the age at marriage in Southeast Asia has changed more modestly—marriage remains nearly universal in some countries. While age at first marriage for females in Japan, Korea, and Taiwan is now close to 30, in Southeast Asia it is substantially younger, remaining close to 20 in a few countries [the Lao People's Democratic Republic (PDR) and Cambodia]. Southeast Asia has much greater diversity in terms of culture and socio-economic development among countries in this region in contrast to East Asia where a high level of homogeneity is found among countries.

Compared to South Asia, Southeast Asia has a higher socio-economic development level and has experienced more rapid family and demographic changes in the past five decades. Hence, in many ways, Southeast Asia stands between East Asia and South Asia in these transitions.

1.2 Explaining Global Family Changes

While a detailed discussion of global family change is out of the scope of this resource book, a brief background is provided here to help users contextualize the family and population changes in Southeast Asia in the past half a century. For a more detailed description, see Yeung et al., (2018).

Global research on patterns of change and stability during an era of socio-economic transformation often draws on two theoretical perspectives. The first emphasizes socio-economic development that transforms the structural conditions under which families are formed. This view argues that industrialization, urbanization, and advancement in education will lead families to converge from more diverse forms of large extended rural-based families to smaller, more egalitarian, and far less stable conjugal families, and the total fertility rate is likely to stabilize at about 3 (Goode, 1963; Parsons, 1942). The second perspective emphasizes changes in people's mindset that transform the notions of how individuals visualize themselves vis-à-vis parents, partners, and children. For example, Lesthaeghe and colleagues have argued that changes in religiosity and secularization in Western countries foster an orientation towards individual growth and gratification, which explains postmodern family behaviour and the prevalence of patterns such as cohabitation, high divorce rates, below-replacement fertility, and non-marital childbearing—what they have labelled the "second demographic transition" (Lesthaeghe & Neels, 2002). This shift of mindset will bring about a stronger emphasis on individual freedom of choice and greater tolerance of diversity in lifestyles. They later hypothesize that such ideational and behavioural changes will spread to other parts of the world (Lesthaeghe, 2010).

In addition to these sweeping factors, when examining family changes in Southeast Asia, it is also important to account for several other moderating factors. While the impact of rapid modernization and related ideational changes are evident, there are also changes—or a lack thereof—that cannot be explained by development and simple ideological changes to increased individualism that can be attributable to historical and cultural factors that have shaped family norms in this region. These factors include the colonial experience of Southeast and South Asian countries, the distinctive nature of kinship patterns and gender inequality in the region, the religious, cultural, and ethnic diversity within and between countries, and different family policies in these countries (see details in Yeung et al., 2018). I briefly mention some of them here.

1.2.1 Historical Context

All countries in Southeast Asia, except Thailand, were under the control of European colonial powers in the nineteenth and early twentieth centuries, some from even earlier. The imposition of foreign legal systems and the identification of certain modes of behaviour as more "modern" undoubtedly influenced local customs and practices in relation to family matters, though it met with considerable resistance in some countries, along with more general nationalist resistance to the colonial imposition of modernity. For example, in Indonesia, it took the form of protests against regulating marriage registration and polygamy (Locher-Scholten, 2000).

During the post-colonial period, defining family and its functions have been a significant part of the nation-building effort in many countries in this region, with a focus on reforms in family law such as changing the laws for the minimum age at marriage, regulating divorce and property settlement, and those controlling polygamy. However, the politicization of family law that began during the colonial era persists, making it difficult to implement these reforms, particularly in countries with religious and ethnic diversity. The tension between the Western and Asian cultures can be observed in family policies in countries in this region. In the Philippines, divorce has been made nearly impossible and access to contraception has been hindered because of the influence of Catholicism dating from the Spanish colonial period. In Singapore, the government proclaimed "family as the basic unit of society" as one element of the core national ideology and stressed the moral value of heterosexual two-parent families and extended families as the cultural ideals that have been embodied in the country's public policies as deliberate protections from the influence of the "Western moral values".

1.2.2 Kinship Patterns

The kinship systems are a basic underpinning of all aspects of family formation and functioning, and that the interplay between social and economic changes in the region explains much of what has been happening in this region. The contrasts between Southeast Asian and East Asian kinship systems are stark. Compared to the highly patriarchal kinship system in East Asia, the kinship system in Southeast Asia is predominantly bilateral, that is, more flexible in matters such as inheritance and post-marriage residential arrangement. Matrilocality, the preference for staying with the wife's parents after the wedding, is clear in most Southeast Asian countries (Bryant, 2002; Guilmoto 2012; Heuveline et al., 2017; Hirschman & Loi, 1996; Zimmer & Kim, 2001). The only exceptions to the bilateral kinship system characterizing most of Southeast Asia are northern Vietnam and the Chinese populations of Singapore and Malaysia, which adhere to a Confucianist system. This bilateral family system may be related to greater gender symmetry in Southeast Asia where females have relatively high autonomy and economic importance in precolonial times (Reid, 1988), and this seems to have persisted in modern times (Booth, 2016). Such kinship system plays a crucial role in the family formation behavior, living arrangements, and caregiving behavior in populations in Southeast Asia.

1.2.3 Cultural Diversity

Another characteristic pertinent to family changes in Southeast Asia is the vast cultural diversity in terms of religion and ethnicity, which results in a variety of ideals for gender and kinship relations. Several countries in Southeast Asia are predominantly Muslims—Brunei, Indonesia, and Malaysia. Buddhism is the main religion in Lao PDR, Cambodia, Myanmar, and Thailand, while the Philippines is mainly Roman Catholic which prohibits divorce and contraceptives. A majority of the Vietnamese have no religion. Most countries contain more than one religious group, with religious composition particularly mixed in Malaysia and Singapore with Islam, Hinduism, Buddhism, Christianity, and others. Ethnic compositions in many countries are also diverse (Yeung et al., 2018). These ethnic and religious beliefs and practices may affect the family formation behaviour in this region. For example, Islamic families have had much higher divorce rate historically than those of other religion and Buddhists are in general more gender egalitarian than other groups.

1.3 Changes in Southeast Asian Families

1.3.1 Changing Marriage Patterns

Southeast Asian countries have historically been characterized by near-universal marriage. Although singlehood rates at ages 30–34 have risen sharply, marriage remains a dominant institution shaping the life course of men and women in most countries although a few countries have rapidly rising singlehood rates. Singapore, for example, currently has the highest proportion of women (about a quarter) who remain single at ages 30–34, followed by Thailand, Brunei, and Myanmar.

The age at marriage has been rising universally. With the age at marriage in this region relatively high to begin with, changes between the 1990s and 2010s have been relatively modest, with the average age at marriage being 22–25 for women and 25–28 for men. Singapore is an exception in this region, with the mean age at marriage being 28 and 30, respectively, for men and women. Divorce rate and cohabitation are relatively low in this region except for a few countries.

1.3.2 Fertility Trends

The fertility rate started to decline more rapidly in Southeast Asia from the 1970s to the end of the 1990s. There are enormous intercountry variations with the TFR in 2015 ranged from 1.2 in Singapore and 1.5 in Thailand to about 3 each in the Philippines and Lao PDR and 5.6 in Timor-Leste. Due to the high fertility rates in the past few decades, the population in this region is relatively young, and most countries have enjoyed demographic dividends. One distinctive characteristic of Southeast Asia is that they have experienced some of the most rapid fertility declines to replacement-level fertility, or near-replacement-level fertility, ever recorded. Singapore, Thailand, and Vietnam fit into this category; Indonesia and Myanmar are not far behind. Singapore's trajectory, in particular, is similar to East Asian countries.

1.3.3 Living Arrangements

Southeast Asia is characterized by its predominantly nuclear families. Back in 1990, more than half of the households in Indonesia, Thailand, and Vietnam were nuclear.

Studies have shown that the nuclear family system in Java dates back to at least the nineteenth century and to as early as the fifteenth century in Vietnam (Schroder-Butterfill, 2004; Schroder-Butterfill & Marianti, 2006). In Southeast Asia, the prevalence of extended families has remained stable over time at 20–40% since the 1970s. In several countries—Thailand, Cambodia, Indonesia, and Vietnam—there has been an increase in the number of extended families in the past decade despite economic growth, which is likely due to the ageing trend. The prevalence of single-parent households remains low in this region. Other family types such as one-person households are on the rise.

1.4 Socio-economic Contexts and Transformation

To contextualize changes in Southeast Asia, some basic developmental indicators from the past few decades for this region are provided. I will briefly highlight the major patterns and trends before delving into each indicator. In general, Southeast Asia has a socio-economic developmental level that lies between East Asia and South Asia.

To begin with, it is important to understand the change in the demographic landscape of this region. Southeast Asia has approximately 640 million people in 2015, accounting for 8.5% of the world population (World Bank, 2015) spread across 11 countries lying east of the Indian subcontinent and south of China. While the countries in this region share some common historical and cultural features, diversity has always been a feature of the region (Hirschman, 2001). Indonesia has the largest population in Southeast Asia, with 258 million people in 2015, or 41% of the region's total population. The Philippines and Vietnam follow at around 100 million people each, and Thailand and Myanmar both have over 50 million people each. There are also several small countries such as Brunei, Timor-Leste, and Singapore.

Economic growth and rise in education countries in Southeast Asia have undergone rapid growth over the past few decades, although the growth rates have been variable. Singapore and Brunei are outliers, and they are now among the world's wealthiest countries. Singapore's gross domestic product (GDP) per capita (purchasing power parity adjusted, in 2011 international dollars) was approximately $80,000 in 2015, significantly higher than the Organisation for Economic Co-operation and Development average of $40,000. Singapore's per-capita GDP has more than doubled in the past two decades, as have those of Malaysia and Thailand, which are currently approximately $25,000 and $15,000, respectively. Indonesia has reached a per-capita income of just over $10,000. The other countries (except Brunei) still have a GDP per capita below $10,000, though they also experienced high growth. This heterogeneity is also reflected in the composition of the respective economies, with agriculture dominating in Myanmar, Cambodia, and Lao PDR, and the manufacturing and service sectors playing important roles in Thailand, the Philippines, Singapore, and Malaysia.

A significant phenomenon observed throughout Southeast Asia is the rapid rise in female educational enrolment rates in all countries. Higher tertiary enrolment rates are related to lower fertility and delayed marriage. Singapore and Thailand experienced very rapid growth in female tertiary enrolment rates, from below 5% in 1970 to 94.5% and 57.3%, respectively, in 2015. Their growth exceeded that of the Philippines, which was well ahead of them in 1970, but its rate nonetheless doubled to 40% in 2015. In most other Southeast Asian countries, significant increases were observed in the mid-1990s, but from a significantly lower base, so that in most of these countries, 30% or fewer young adults are currently enrolled in tertiary education.

Gender inequality and labour market opportunities for women in Southeast Asia are characterized by a high, though declining, level of gender inequality in many countries although, in general, Southeast Asian countries have lower gender inequality than those in East Asia and South Asia. Singapore has the lowest level of gender inequality, followed by Malaysia. The trend in the female labour force participation rate (FLFPR) affects the family system significantly. Although we typically expect a U-shaped curve of female employment, with more women employed in agricultural economies, a decline in the FLFPR with economic growth, and then a rise in the FLFPR as services emerge, we do not always see this pattern in this region (Dasgupta & Verick, 2017). Cambodia, Lao PDR, Myanmar, and Vietnam have had a persistently high FLFPR of approximately 80% since 1990. Thailand also had a high FLFPR (76%) in 1990, but it has declined to the current level of 63%.

The rapid socio-economic transformations, together with evolving cultural norms and values, have led to changes in family life in Southeast Asia as reflected in fertility, marriage, family structure, and intergenerational relations. The great variations in the levels and trends of these family demographic changes also reflect the cultural, historical background mentioned above and family and related social policies such as the family planning programs and family and social policies in each country. The following sections describe each indicator chosen in this brief.

1.5 Highlights of the Trends and Patterns

The following are some of the key areas that have gone through significant transformation:

1.5.1 Population

- The region's population has expanded to as much as thrice its size in 1970. Five of the Southeast Asian countries are now among the world's 20 most populous countries with Indonesia taking the lead as the 3th most populous country in the world. The population density in countries such as Singapore, Vietnam, and the Philippines has risen exponentially.

- Life expectancy has risen by 20 years on average in 50 years. Singapore has the highest life expectancy at birth in the region at 82.6 years, while Myanmar has the lowest at 65.9 years.
- Most Southeast Asian countries are starting to age gradually. However, in Singapore, Thailand, and Vietnam, the proportion of 65-year-olds and above, as well as the oldest old (aged 80 and above), are rising exponentially. In 2015, the old-age dependency ratio in Singapore and Thailand were 16.1 and 14.6, respectively, higher than the world average of 12.6.
- Conversely, the child dependency ratio in the region has been declining, though the population remains relatively young. The majority of the countries have child dependency ratios that are higher than the world average of 39.7.

1.5.2 Socio-economic Development

- GDP in the region has grown with varying trajectories across the countries. Singapore has shown substantive growth in terms of GDP per capita increasing from US$30,000 to US$55,237 in the time span of 1998–2017. On the other end of the spectrum, countries like Cambodia and Timor-Leste experienced the lowest rates of GDP per capita during the same period.
- Poverty incidence has generally declined in the region. Significant reductions in poverty levels were seen in Vietnam, Cambodia, Lao PDR, and Thailand where the poverty headcount ratios were cut by about 35–75% within fifteen years. Timor-Leste, on the other hand, experienced increased poverty rates from 36.3% in 2001 to 41.8% in 2014.
- Singapore and Thailand have the largest proportion of highly educated people, with Singapore having around 90% and Thailand with 50% of their population obtaining tertiary education. In contrast, Lao PDR has the least number of people going to the tertiary level with just a 17% enrolment rate in 2015, and Malaysia has seen a decline in tertiary enrolment from 37% in 2010 to 29% in 2015.
- Women's participation in paid labour has been high in Southeast Asia, but increased engagement of women in paid work was more pronounced in Brunei and Singapore. Meanwhile, the opposite trend was observed in Thailand and Timor-Leste.

1.5.3 Union Formation and Dissolution

- Marked changes have occurred in the family formation behaviour of the population in Southeast Asia. Comparing with the 1970s, marriage rates seem to have risen in the region except in Timor-Leste. But when comparing with the 1980s and the 1990s, significantly fewer Thais, Singaporeans, and Bruneians are getting married nowadays. On the other hand, more Indonesians and Filipinos are tying the knot.

- Generally, those who get married tend to do so at a later age. Notable exceptions are Indonesia, Vietnam, and Cambodia where the singulated mean ages at marriage (SMAM) have recently gone down. A significantly higher number of women and men in their late 30s are also remaining single particularly in Myanmar, Singapore, and Thailand.
- Available data show divorce rates are increasing in Singapore, Thailand, and Brunei, but decreasing in Indonesia and Vietnam.
- Consensual unions or cohabitations also warrant attention, particularly in the Philippines and Thailand where 20–40% of women 20–24 years old and more than 10% of men 25–29 years old are cohabiting.

1.5.4 Childbearing

- Generally, fertility rates in the region have significantly declined although the majority (six out of eleven) of the countries still have TFRs that are above or around the fertility replacement level. Interestingly, the majority of the countries also have had a decreasing mean age at childbearing (MAC) which translates to women giving birth at an earlier age. We however see a pattern where those with decreasing MAC are associated with lower GDP countries while higher GDP countries have increasing or little change in MAC. Outliers here are Brunei (high GDP but little change in MAC) and Myanmar (low GDP but increasing MAC).
- Age-specific fertility rates (ASFRs) show that the peak of childbearing for high-fertility countries is from the early to late 20s, and late 20s to early 30s for low-fertility countries. Over the years, fertility rates for women in their 20s and early 30s are lower now compared to the 1970s.
- The incidence of teenage pregnancy as measured by adolescent fertility rates has also gone down for the past 50 years. Exceptions here are Vietnam and the Philippines which manifested recent increases in adolescent fertility rates of around 10% points in the past 14 and 19 years, respectively.
- Childlessness is now higher in Cambodia and Indonesia and has escalated by 16% in Singapore since the 1970s. On the other hand, Thailand and Vietnam have fewer childless women in the same age group.
- Generally, actual fertility rates are higher compared with ideal rates except for Singapore where the reverse pattern was observed.

1.5.5 Household Structure

- Household sizes have fallen universally at different levels, with Singapore having the smallest households at 3.5 persons per household and Lao PDR the biggest at 5.9 persons per household.

1.5 Highlights of the Trends and Patterns

- Nuclear households with children are still the most common type of household in the region although the recent trend shows a decreasing pattern, with only Malaysia moving contrary to this trend. In comparison, the percentage of nuclear households with no children is rising although the numbers remain below 6% for all countries, except for Singapore where figures reached 13.7% in 2010.
- Extended family households remain pervasive in Southeast Asia with most countries having more than 25% of this type of household. In Indonesia and Malaysia, extended households are decreasing but in Thailand, Cambodia, Indonesia, and Vietnam, the percentages are increasing.
- Single-parent households, which are less than 8% of households in each of the countries, are generally decreasing except in Thailand and the Philippines. This downward trend is similarly observed for composite households which are less common than single-parent households.
- One-person households are gradually rising, despite accounting for around 2% or below of all households in each country. In Singapore, there is an exponential increase in households consisting of those who live alone, from 6% in 1980 to 12.2% in 2010.

1.5.6 Education

- Most countries have reached full enrolment at the primary level with the rate of out-of-school children of primary school age being below 5%.
- There is a gradual increase of adults aged 25 and above having completed upper secondary since 2000. Among countries having at least upper secondary education in 2014, Singapore has the highest rate at 70%, while Indonesia has less than half the rate at 30%. Cambodia has the lowest rates in the region with below 10% in 2009.
- The rate of the adults above 25 years of age having completed at least tertiary education is much lower, with Singapore having the highest rate of 40% and Indonesia with consistent rates of below 10%.
- Tertiary enrolment rates in the region are generally converging to reach gender parity. Nevertheless, female enrolment rates in tertiary education are consistently higher than that for males in half of the countries in the region, namely Brunei, Malaysia, Myanmar Thailand, and the Philippines.

1.5.7 Youth Unemployment

- Southeast Asia has the world's highest youth unemployment rates, and female unemployment is especially high for Indonesia at 21%, and Timor-Leste and the Philippines at 17% in 2015. In comparison, male unemployment does not exceed 10% throughout the 25 years from 1990 to 2015.

1.5.8 Child Health

- Overweight—The prevalence of overweight children is growing, especially in Thailand and Indonesia having the highest rates of 11% in 2014.
- The prevalence of wasting is high in Timore-Leste, Lao PDR, Cambodia and Indonesia.

References

Booth, A. (2016). Women, work and the family: Is Southeast Asia different? *Economic History of Developing Regions, 31*(1), 167. https://doi.org/10.1080/20780389.2015.1132624

Bryant, J. (2002). Patrilines, patrilocality and fertility decline in Viet Nam. *Asia-Pacific Population Journal, 17*, 111–128.

Dasgupta, S., & Verick, S. S. (Eds.). (2017). *Transformation of Women at Work in Asia: An Unfinished Development Agenda*. Los Angeles: Sage.

Dommaraju, P., & Jones, G. (2011). Divorce trends in Asia. *Asian Journal of Social Science, 39*(6), 725–750. https://doi.org/10.1163/156853111X619201

Goode, W. J. (1963). *World revolution and family patterns*. New York: Free Press.

Guilmoto, C. Z. (2012). Son preference, sex selection, and kinship in Vietnam. *Population and Development Review, 38*, 31–54.

Heuveline, P., Demont, F., Poch, B. (2017). *The transition to adulthood in Cambodia*. Population Working Papers PWP-CCPR-2012–016, California Center Population Research University, California, Los Angeles.

Hirschman, C., & Loi, V. M. (1996). Family and household structure in Vietnam: some glimpses from a recent survey. *Pacific Affairs, 69*, 229–249.

Hirschman, C. (2001). Fertility transition: Southeast Asia A2. In N. J. Smelser & P. B. Baltes (Eds.), *International encyclopedia of the social & behavioral sciences* (pp. 5597–5602). Oxford: Pergamon.

Jones, G. W. (1997). Modernization and divorce: Contrasting trends in Islamic Southeast Asia and the West. *Population and Development Review, 23*(1), 95–114.

Jones, G. W. (2012). Marriage migration in Asia: An introduction. *Asian and Pacific Migration Journal, 21*(3), 287–290. https://doi.org/10.1177/011719681202100301

Jones, G., & Shen, H.-H. (2008). International marriage in East and Southeast Asia: Trends and research emphases. *Citizenship Studies, 12*(1), 9–25. https://doi.org/10.1080/13621020701794091

Jones, G. W., & Yeung, W.-J.J. (2014). Marriage in Asia. *Journal of Family Issues, 35*(12), 1567–1583.

Lesthaeghe, R. (2010). The unfolding story of the second demographic transition. *Population Development Review, 36*, 211–251.

Lesthaeghe, R., & Neels, K. (2002). From the first to the second demographic transition: an interpretation of the spatial continuity of demographic innovation in France, Belgium and Switzerland. *European Journal of Population/Revue européenne de démographie, 18*, 325–60.

Locher-Scholten, E. (2000). *Women and the Colonial State: Essays on Gender and Modernity in the Netherlands Indies, 1900–1942*. Amsterdam: Amsterdam University Press.

Parsons, T. (1942). Age and sex in the social structure of the United States. *American Sociological Review, 7*, 604–616.

Raymo, J. M., Park, H., Xie, Y., & Yeung, W. J. J. (2015). Marriage and family in East Asia: Continuity and change. *Annual Review of Sociology, 41*, 471–492.

References

Reid, A. (1988). Southeast Asia in the age of commerce. In *The lands below the winds* (vol. 1, pp. 1450–1680). Yale University Press.

Schroder-Butterfill, E. (2004). Inter-generational family support provided by older people in Indonesia. *Ageing and Society, 24*, 497–530.

Schroder-Butterfill, E., & Marianti, R. (2006). A framework for understanding old-age vulnerabilities. *Ageing and Society, 26*, 9–35.

World Bank. (2015). *Health nutrition and population statistics*. Retrieved from http://databank.worldbank.org/data/reports.aspx?source=health-nutrition-and-population-statistics&preview=on

Yeung, W. J. J., Desai, S., & Jones, G. W. (2018). Families in southeast and South Asia. *Annual Review of Sociology, 44*, 469–495.

Yeung, W.J. J., & Hu S. (2018). *Family and Population Changes in Singapore: A Unique Case in Global Family Change*. Routledge: London and New York.

Zimmer, Z., Kim, S. K. (2001). Living arrangements and socio-demographic conditions of older adults in Cambodia. *Journal of Cross-Cultural Gerontology, 16*, 353–381

Open Access This chapter is licensed under the terms of the Creative Commons Attribution 4.0 International License (http://creativecommons.org/licenses/by/4.0/), which permits use, sharing, adaptation, distribution and reproduction in any medium or format, as long as you give appropriate credit to the original author(s) and the source, provide a link to the Creative Commons license and indicate if changes were made.

The images or other third party material in this chapter are included in the chapter's Creative Commons license, unless indicated otherwise in a credit line to the material. If material is not included in the chapter's Creative Commons license and your intended use is not permitted by statutory regulation or exceeds the permitted use, you will need to obtain permission directly from the copyright holder.

Chapter 2
Trends in Population and Socioeconomic Development in Southeast Asia

Southeast Asia is composed of 631.7 million people (World Bank, 2015) spread across 11 countries that lie east of the Indian continent and south of China. Geographically, insular Southeast Asia includes Brunei, Timor-Leste (East Timor), Indonesia, Malaysia, the Philippines, and Singapore while Cambodia, Lao PDR, Myanmar (Burma), Thailand, and Vietnam comprise mainland Southeast Asia. Collectively, countries in the region share common features in terms of geography, history, and culture, yet diversity has always been part of the region's defining features (Hirschman, 2001). This section shows changes in Southeast Asian countries' populations from 1960 to 2015.

2.1 Population Structure of Southeast Asia

Population Size. Figure 2.1 shows that all countries have experienced substantial population growth (2–3 times) during this period. Indonesia has the largest population in the region which consistently grew since the 1960s. By 2015, Indonesia's population was 257.6 million which accounts for 41% of the region's population. Other countries with large populations are the Philippines (100.7 million), Vietnam (91.7 million), Thailand (68.0 million), Myanmar (53.9 million), Malaysia (30.3 million), and Cambodia (15.6 million) in 2015. The Philippines and Vietnam are also among the fastest-growing countries.

Small population countries are Brunei (423,000), Timor-Leste (1.2 million), Singapore (5.5 million), and Lao PDR (6.8 million), whose individual population sizes only account for 1% of the region's aggregate population.

People Aged 65 and above. Referring to Fig. 2.2, there is a general increasing trend of the older adults population aged 65 and above in the region echoing the global ageing trend. From a range of 2.0%–4.7% of the population in 1960, most countries have seen a gradual increase between 0.5 and 3 percentage points in 2015. Exceptions are Singapore and Thailand which have seen steep increases in the 65 and above

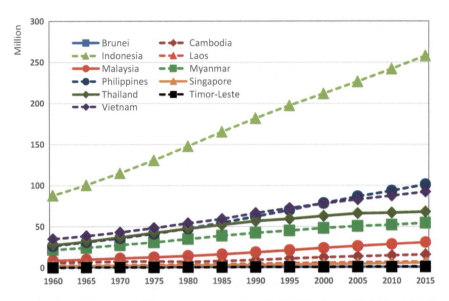

Fig. 2.1 Total population of Southeast Asian countries, 1960–2015. *Source* World Bank health nutrition and population statistics accessed on 25 October 2016

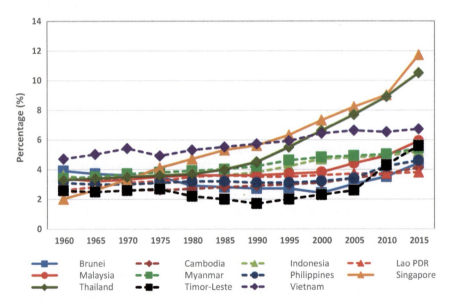

Fig. 2.2 Percentage of total population aged 65 and above in Southeast Asia, 1960–2015. *Source* United Nations, Department of Economic and Social Affairs, Population Division (2015). World Population Prospects: The 2015 Revision, accessed on 6 January 2017

population by 9.2% and 7.2%, respectively, in 55 years. For Timor-Leste, its elderly population has grown by 3% in just a decade, from 2005 to 2015. Singapore has experienced one of the world's most rapid ageing trends as reflected from a change from 2% in 1960 to 12% in 2015 and a drastic jump of 2.7% in only five years, from 2010 to 2015. According to the recent World Health Organization (WHO) report on Ageing and Health (2015), the two main drivers of population ageing are the increasing life expectancy owing to the burgeoning socioeconomic development on a global scale, and the falling fertility rates. Most countries in this region, other than Singapore and Thailand, remain relatively young, especially Lao PDR, Cambodia, and Brunei.

Old-age dependency ratio. The World Bank defines the old-age dependency ratio (OADR) as the ratio of older dependents (people older than 64) to the working-age population (15–64). Data shown are the change in the proportion of dependents per 100 working-age population. It should be noted, however, that while OADR is a common measure used to determine the dependency of older people to the working-age population, using this indicator in Southeast Asia where the context of ageing in terms of retirement and pension schemes is different from Europe, may render an inaccurate picture of old-age dependency ratio in the region. Besides, OADR is an outdated and misleading indicator as these days a large number of those who are older than 64 are in good health and remain productive in the labour force or in other ways.

Figure 2.3 indicates that an increase over time with Singapore and Thailand showing the most rapid growth. In 2015, OADR is highest in Singapore (16.1) and Thailand (14.6) implying that compared with other countries in Southeast Asia, the working-age population in these two countries will bear the most strain in trying to support their older population. OADRs in these countries are higher than the world average of 12.6. Excluding Timor-Leste which has an OADR of 10.7, the rest of Southeast Asia have a gradual growth and OADRs below 10 in 2015.

Child dependency ratio. Conversely, the child dependency ratio is the ratio of the population aged 0–14 to the population aged 15–64 and presented as the number of dependents per 100 persons of working age (15–64).

Figure 2.4 shows that the child dependency ratio in the region has been declining in all countries except Timor-Leste, where the child dependency ratio has recently increased from 75.8 in 2010 to 81.5 in 2015, which is the highest in Southeast Asia. The rest of the Southeast Asian countries showed a decline in child dependency ratios from 1980 onwards, the time when they started experiencing fertility decline. Singapore's significant decline started a decade earlier, from 67 in 1970 to 39.7 in 1980. By 2015, Singapore's child dependency ratio reached 24.7 and was the lowest in the region reflecting its early and rapid decline in fertility rate.

Aside from Timor-Leste, the rest of Southeast Asia have child dependency ratios lower than 60 but countries such as Lao PDR, the Philippines, Cambodia, Myanmar, and Indonesia have rates that are higher than the world average of 39.7 and Southeast Asia's average of 39.3.

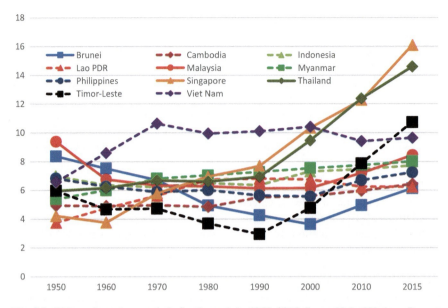

Fig. 2.3 Old-age dependency ratio in Southeast Asia, 1950–2015. *Source* United Nations, Department of Economic and Social Affairs, Population Division (2015). World Population Prospects: The 2015 Revision, accessed on 6 January 2017

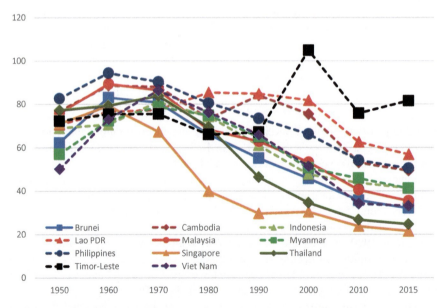

Fig. 2.4 Child dependency ratio in Southeast Asia, 1950–2015. *Source* United Nations, Department of Economic and Social Affairs, Population Division (2015). World Population Prospects: The 2015 Revision, accessed on 17 March 2017

2.1 Population Structure of Southeast Asia

The proportion of the oldest-old Population. The proportion of oldest old, or those 80 years and above, requires a significantly higher level of healthcare, especially long-term care, due to a more dramatic decline in physical and cognitive functioning. Thus, its increase warrants special attention. It has been on a gradual rise in Southeast Asia for the past 60 years (Fig. 2.5). Notable exceptions from this trend are Singapore, Thailand, and Vietnam where the number of people over 80 years old has been rising in exponential proportions. In Singapore for example, the percentage of the oldest old has risen from 0.5% in 1980 to 2.4% in 2015 representing an almost quadruple increase in 35 years. A similar rapid rise is also seen in Thailand and Vietnam. Meanwhile, the rest of the countries remained below 1% in 2015, from below 0.5% in 1950. It should be noted that countries should be prepared as the ageing trend will be rapid in the next few decades due to the sharp decline in fertility and many of the countries in this region may not have adequate financial resources or infrastructure ready for caring for a fast growing group of older adults.

Life expectancy. The United Nations defines life expectancy at birth as the number of years a newborn infant would live if prevailing patterns of mortality at the time of its birth were to stay the same throughout its life.

Looking more closely at life expectancy in Southeast Asia in Fig. 2.6, countries in Southeast Asia have made significant progress in improving life expectancies at birth from about 33–65 years in 1960 to about 65–82 years in 2015. Timor-Leste in particular has more than doubled its life expectancy from 33.7 years in 1960 to

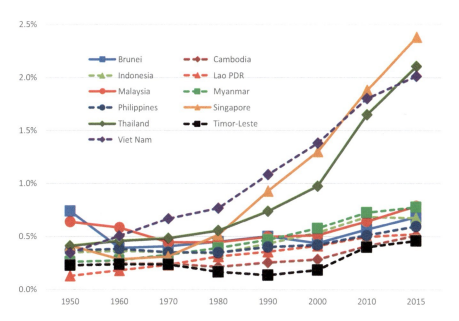

Fig. 2.5 Proportion of oldest old in Southeast Asia, 1950–2015. *Source* United Nations, Department of Economic and Social Affairs, Population Division (2015). World Population Prospects: The 2015 Revision, accessed on 17 March 2017

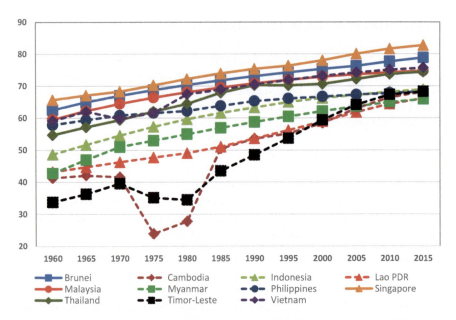

Fig. 2.6 Life expectancy at birth in Southeast Asia, 1960–2015. *Source* World Bank, World Development Indicators accessed on 6 January 2017. *Note* Data are from 2014

75.6 in 2015. Cambodia, Myanmar, Laos, and Indonesia have also increased their life expectancy at birth by more than 20 years. Except for deviations in the 1970s and early 1980s in Cambodia caused by the genocide and Timor-Leste caused by the Indonesian invasion of East Timor respectively, life expectancies in all countries have consistently risen in the past 45 years.

In 2015, Singapore has the highest life expectancy at 82.6 years and is the only country to have a life expectancy above 80 years, followed by Brunei at 78.8 years. This corresponds to the high levels of economic and technological developments that Brunei and Singapore have experienced being the wealthiest in the region, which has resulted in more people living into adulthood, thereby increasing life expectancy. Malaysia, Thailand, and Vietnam have relatively high life expectancies at 74.7, 74.4, and 75.6 years, respectively, in 2015. Within the entire region in 2015, Myanmar has the lowest life expectancy at 65.9 years. Lao PDR has a similar level of life expectancy.

2.2 Population Density

In terms of population density, countries in the region are generally becoming more densely populated although Vietnam, Thailand, and Myanmar have shown indications that the rise in population density seems to be slowing recently.

2.2 Population Density

Singapore is the most densely populated country, and with the most rapid rate of increase over time, in the region. In 2015, it has approximately 7,828 people per square kilometre (see Fig. 2.7a). This is because despite the country's relatively small population size when compared with its regional counterparts, Singapore is the smallest country in Southeast Asia with a total land area of 707 square kilometres and

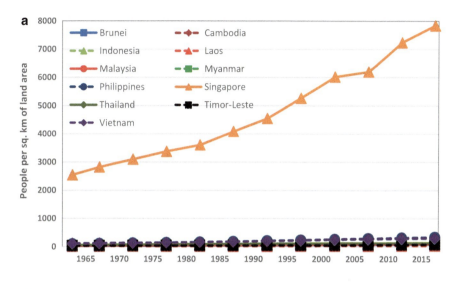

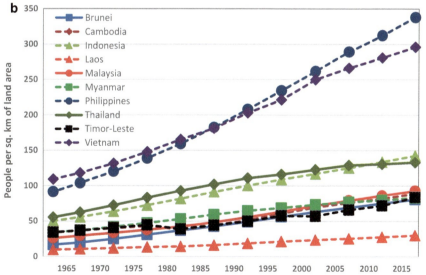

Fig. 2.7 a Population density of Southeast Asian countries, 1960–2015, b population density of Southeast Asian countries excluding Singapore, 1960–2015. *Source* World Bank, World Development Indicators accessed on 01 December 2016

closely resembles the size of Indonesia's and Philippines' capital cities of Jakarta and Manila. Its population density grew rapidly from the 1960s until the current period, matching the rapid growth of its economy and development.

The Philippines and Vietnam are also densely populated with approximately 337 and 295 people per square kilometre in 2015 (see Fig. 2.7b). These numbers are notably higher than the population density of the rest of the countries in the region. Laos PDR is the most sparsely populated country.

2.3 Level of Economic Development

Looking at GDP per capita as an indicator of economic development, Fig. 2.8a shows that countries in Southeast Asia are on an upward trend for the past twenty-five years with some countries progressing more rapidly than others. Singapore and Brunei are the wealthiest in the region with GDPs per capita of US$80,000 and $60,000, respectively, in 2015. GDP per capita in these countries is significantly higher than the OECD average of US$40,000. Singapore's GDP per capita enjoyed the sharpest increase, more than doubled in the past two decades, while Brunei's GDP per capita has been on a gradual decline since 1995. Malaysia and Thailand also experienced accelerated growth in the last two decades with GDPs per capita growing by more than 100%, jumping above ASEAN's[1] average albeit still lower than the OECD's average. In 1992, these four countries together with the Philippines and Indonesia (known as the ASEAN 6) established the ASEAN Free Trade Agreement which allowed for low or no-tariff trade within the region. Figure 2.8b shows that under the ASEAN 6, Indonesia had the fastest growth, only the Philippines and Indonesia have GDPs per capita that are below the ASEAN average although Indonesia's GDP also doubled from US$4,477 in 1990 to US$10,385 in 2015, compared to the Philippines' GDP per capita which only grew by 73% within the same period. Recently, Vietnam, Lao PDR, and Cambodia are also experiencing steady growth in GDP per capita while Timor-Leste is trailing behind.

Consistent with GDP per capita growth is the decline of poverty in the region. Figure 2.9 shows that at the turn of the century, Lao PDR, Cambodia, Thailand, and Timor-Leste still had poverty rates between 40 and 50%. But by 2010, the rates dropped to less than 30% and continued to decline till 2015. Timor-Leste is an exception where poverty rates grew from 36.3% in 2001 to 41.8% in 2014. Relatively little is known about Timor-Leste due to the availability and accuracy of the data; thus, it is difficult to interpret the trends in this country.

Dramatic reductions in poverty were observed in several countries. In Vietnam, poverty rates were cut by 35% in four years, and in Cambodia, rates went down by 65% in nine years. In addition, Thailand and Lao PDR experienced a drop in poverty rates by 75% and 41%, respectively, within fifteen years. In comparison,

---

[1] ASEAN refers to the Association of Southeast Asian Nations which includes all ten countries in Southeast Asia except Timor-Leste. Source: www.asean.org.

2.3 Level of Economic Development

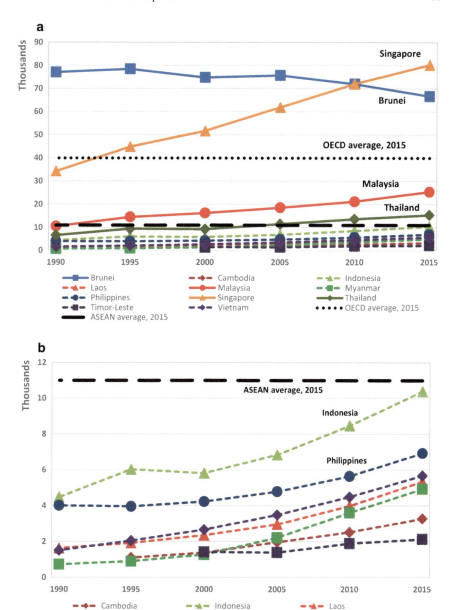

Fig. 2.8 **a** GDP per capita of Southeast Asian countries, 1990–2015, **b** GDP per capita of Southeast Asian countries excluding Singapore, Brunei, Malaysia and Thailand, 1990–2015. *Source* World Bank, World Development Indicators accessed on 01 December 2016. *Note* Figures for GDP PPP per capita are based on constant 2011 international $

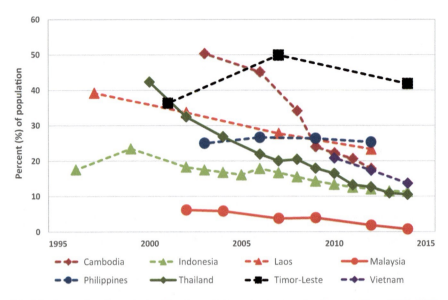

Fig. 2.9 Poverty headcount ratio of Southeast Asian countries at national poverty lines, 1995–2015. *Source* World Bank, World Development Indicators accessed on 01 December 2016. *Note* Data for Brunei, Myanmar, and Singapore not available

poverty reduction occurred more gradually in Malaysia, Indonesia, and the Philippines. Beyond 2010, Malaysia had the lowest poverty rate in the region (excluding Singapore). Timor-Leste had the highest poverty rate which poses a tremendous challenge to meet the development goals with increasing demand for schools, jobs, health, food, and other infrastructure facilities.

2.4 Education

Southeast Asia has had substantial improvements in education. Looking at the gross tertiary-level enrolment rates in Fig. 2.10a, we see that except for the Philippines which already had a 17.6% tertiary enrolment rate in 1970, all of Southeast Asia started with a 5% tertiary enrolment rate in 1970 before jumping to more than 30% by 2015, close to the world average of 34.5% (World Bank, 2014a), with significant increases mostly observed in the middle of the 1990s. The countries leading this trend are Singapore and Thailand where tertiary enrolment rates surged to 89.5% and 52.5% in 2015, respectively from below 10%.

The Philippines on the other hand moved at a slower pace from a 17% enrolment rate in the 1970s to 35% in 2015. Lao PDR has the least number of people going to the tertiary level with just a 17% enrolment rate in 2015. Its rates also show signs of stalling since 2010. One notable trend in the chart is the decline in tertiary enrolment

2.4 Education

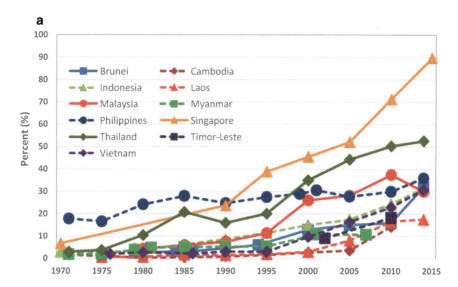

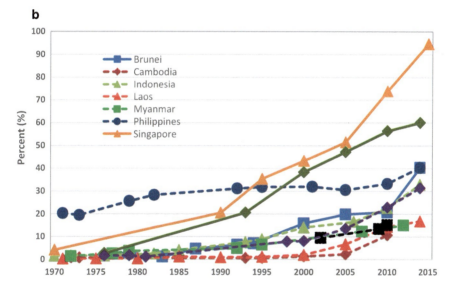

Fig. 2.10 a Gross tertiary enrolment ratio in Southeast Asia for both sexes, 1970–2015, **b** gross tertiary enrolment ratio for females in Southeast Asia, 1970–2015. *Source* World Bank, World Development Indicators accessed on 01 December 2016 except for Singapore. Data for Singapore are from http://data.gov.sg, accessed on 7 December 2016. *Note* Data not available for Malaysia

for Malaysia in 2015. From 4% in 1980, Malaysia's enrolment ratio rose to 37% in 2010 but went down to 29.7% in 2015.

Achievements in women's education in the region mirror the general pattern of tertiary enrolment for both genders (Fig. 2.10b). The ratio of women reaching the tertiary level is on an upward trend with Singapore and Thailand rising faster than the rest of the countries in the region. Singapore has the highest tertiary enrolment ratio at 94.5%, almost thrice the ratio of most countries in Southeast Asia. It also showed the most dramatic improvement, rising from 6.48% in 1970 to its current rate, highlighting an increase of more than 1200% in 45 years. Figure 2.10b also shows that generally, female enrolment at the tertiary level is higher than the enrolment ratio for both genders with differences that could go as much as 8 percentage points such as in Brunei where the female tertiary enrolment rate is 40.1% compared to both gender's enrolment rate at 31.7%. The majority of the countries' female enrolment ratios are also above 30%, close to the world and East Asia's average of 35% and significantly higher than South Asia's average of 21% (World Bank, 2014b).

2.5 Female Labour Force Participation

With regard to women's participation in the workforce, two general groupings tend to manifest: the CLMV[2] and ASEAN-6 although Timor-Leste and Thailand are the outliers in those groupings (Fig. 2.11). Starting from 76 to 84% rates in the 1990s, about 80% of working-age women in CLMV countries participated in the labour force. Booth (2016) suggested that the unusually high female participation rates in these countries are rooted in their socialist past which compelled women to join the workforce, coupled with high mortality rates among men during the Indochina wars. High participation rates were carried over in the 1990s with the creation of more employment opportunities in the labour-intensive manufacturing and service sectors (p. 182).

ASEAN-6 countries have lower female labour force participation rates and the numbers are more heterogeneous ranging from 47 to 65% in 2015. Participation rates in ASEAN-6 countries are also more comparable to the world average of 50%, OECD average of 63%, and East Asia and the Pacific's average of 61%. In the whole of Southeast Asia, Cambodia has the highest FLFPR at 82% while Timor-Leste has the lowest at 25%. Collectively, Southeast Asian women are actively participating in the labour force compared with South Asia where only a third of working-age women do so.

---

[2] CLMV is an informal subgrouping in ASEAN which refers to the less-developed economies in the region. The acronym stands for Cambodia, Lao PDR, Myanmar, and Vietnam.

2.6 Gender Inequality Index (GII)

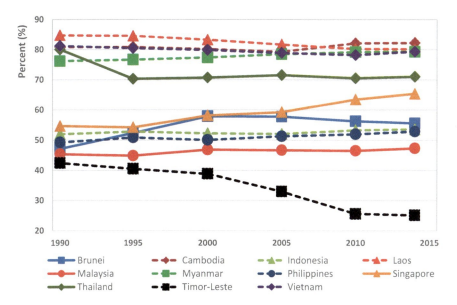

Fig. 2.11 Female labour force participation rate in Southeast Asia, 1990–2015. *Source* World Bank, World Development Indicators accessed on 01 December 2016

2.6 Gender Inequality Index (GII)

The Gender Inequality Index (GII) is a composite measure of gender inequality using three dimensions: reproductive health, (political) empowerment, and the labour market. A lower GII value is indicative of lesser inequality between women and men. As shown in Fig. 2.12, gender inequality in Southeast Asian countries has generally decreased over the past 20 years, with the largest decreases observed for Cambodia and Singapore. The data for Lao PDR and Myanmar are only available from the years 2000 and 2010, respectively. Singapore has consistently had the lowest GII across 20 years, from 0.25 in 1995 and a brief increase to 0.27 in 2000, which followed a rapid decrease to 0.07 in 2015. Singapore experienced the least gender inequality not solely in the region but is among the lowest globally and ranked 5th in 2015 according to the United Nations Human Development Report, jointly with Denmark (Programme, 2016).

Although Cambodia is still experiencing one of the highest GII values in Southeast Asia, the rate of decline has been comparable to Singapore with a decrease of 0.18 over 2 decades, from 0.66 in 1995 to 0.48 in 2015. In contrast, the GII in the Philippines was considerably lower at 0.48 in 1995 compared to Cambodia, however, inequality in the former country decreased at a much slower pace to 0.44 in 2015. Indonesia and Lao PDR follow closely behind Cambodia and are decreasing at similar rates over the years, from 0.57 in 2000 to 0.47 in 2015.

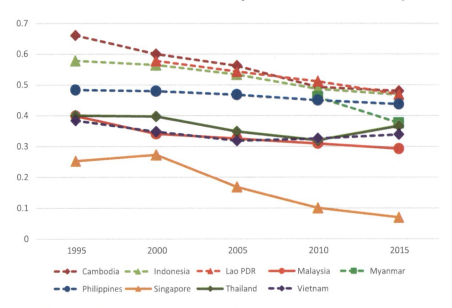

Fig. 2.12 Gender Inequality Index (GII) in Southeast Asia, 1990–2015. *Source* United Nations Development Programme, Human Development Data accessed on 05 May 2017. *Note* No information available for Brunei and Timor-Leste. Information on Lao PDR and Myanmar only available from 2000 to 2010 respectively

The gender inequality trends for Thailand and Vietnam over the years differ from the rest of the Southeast Asian countries, as recent increases in inequality have been observed. Thailand's GII declined from 0.40 in 1995 to 0.32 in 2010 but increased to 0.37 in 2015. Similarly, the GII in Vietnam decreased from 0.38 in 1995 to 0.32 in 2005 but gradually increased over the next decade to 0.34 in 2015. The reasons for these increases are not clear and warrant further investigation.

References

Booth, A. (2016). Women, work and the family: Is Southeast Asia different? *Economic History of Developing Regions, 31*(1), 167. https://doi.org/10.1080/20780389.2015.1132624

Hirschman, C. (2001). Fertility transition: Southeast Asia A2. In N. J. Smelser & P. B. Baltes (Eds.), *International encyclopedia of the social & behavioral sciences* (pp. 5597–5602). Pergamon.

Programme, U. N. D. (2016). *Human developments Reports*. Retrieved from http://hdr.undp.org/en/composite/GII#c

United Nations. (2015). *World fertility Patterns 2015*. Retrieved from New York http://www.un.org/en/development/desa/population/publications/pdf/fertility/world-fertility-patterns-2015.pdf

WHO. (2015). Pertussis vaccines: WHO position paper—August 2015. *Weekly Epidemiological Record, 35*(90), 433–460.

World Bank. (2014a). Gross enrolment ratio, tertiary, both sexes.

World Bank. (2014b). School enrolment, tertiary, female.

References

World Bank. (2015). *Health nutrition and population statistics.* Retrieved from http://databank.worldbank.org/data/reports.aspx?source=health-nutrition-and-population-statistics&preview=on

Open Access This chapter is licensed under the terms of the Creative Commons Attribution 4.0 International License (http://creativecommons.org/licenses/by/4.0/), which permits use, sharing, adaptation, distribution and reproduction in any medium or format, as long as you give appropriate credit to the original author(s) and the source, provide a link to the Creative Commons license and indicate if changes were made.

The images or other third party material in this chapter are included in the chapter's Creative Commons license, unless indicated otherwise in a credit line to the material. If material is not included in the chapter's Creative Commons license and your intended use is not permitted by statutory regulation or exceeds the permitted use, you will need to obtain permission directly from the copyright holder.

Chapter 3
Marriage

3.1 Singulate Mean Age at Marriage (SMAM)

The singulate mean age at marriage (SMAM) refers to the average length of a single life expressed in years among those who marry before 50 years old. Figure 3.1a, b show that increasingly more men and women in the region are marrying later, although there are also indications in recent years that some choose to marry earlier.

Countries such as Singapore, Myanmar, Thailand, the Philippines, and Lao PDR show a rise in SMAM across genders, with males generally marrying two to three years older than females. Historically, Singaporeans marry at the latest age in the region regardless of gender and they marry two to three years later than their Burmese and Malaysian counterparts. However, the trend for Myanmar illustrates a faster rise in SMAM compared to Singapore. In 40 years, Myanmar's SMAM for women rose by 4.8 years compared to Singapore's 3.7 years (Fig. 3.1a). The rise in SMAM for Myanmar was even faster for men with a 3.7-year increase in 3.5 decades compared to Singapore's 2.6 years in four decades (Fig. 3.1b). It is interesting to note that these two countries have the highest SMAMs in the region and show similar trends despite very different levels of economic development, educational attainment among its population, religious and ethnic composition, and women's labour force participation rate suggesting that the relationship of these elements with marriage is more complex than what is conventionally understood.

Thailand has also been showing a steady and steep increase in SMAM for men, with a rise of 2.7 years in more than three decades, around 1.1 years higher than what the Philippines has experienced in four decades. Within the same period, the same trend was observed for women where Thailand's SMAM increased by 2.1 years, about 0.5 years higher than the Philippines' 1.6-year increase.

The rising age at marriage was also evident in Lao PDR. The latest data show that for men, SMAM increased from 23.9 in 1995 to 24.7 in 2005 (Fig. 3.1b); while for women, SMAM increased from 21.2 to 21.7 within the same period (Fig. 3.1a). Among the cluster of countries with rising SMAM, Lao PDR has the youngest age

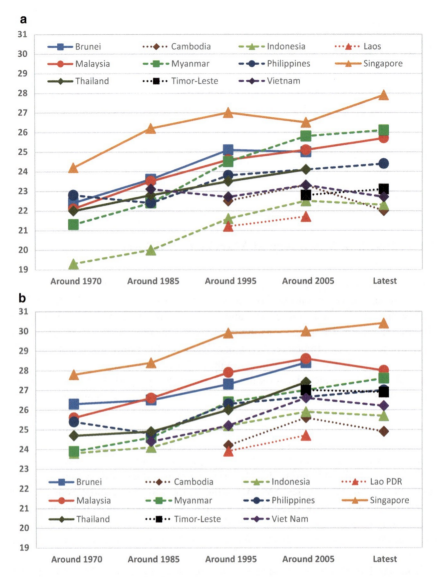

Fig. 3.1 **a** SMAM for females in Southeast Asia, around 1970–2010, **b** SMAM for males in Southeast Asia, around 1970–2010. *Source* UN World Marriage Data 2012, accessed on 26 October 2016. *Notes* "Around 1970" data for Brunei and Indonesia refer to 1971, for Myanmar to 1973. "Around 1985" data for Indonesia, Malaysia, Philippines, and Singapore refer to 1980, for Brunei to 1981, for Myanmar to 1983, for Vietnam to 1989. "Around 1995" data for Indonesia, Philippines and Singapore refer to 1990, for Brunei, Malaysia and Myanmar to 1991, for Cambodia to 1998, for Vietnam to 1999. "Around 2005" data for Indonesia, Malaysia, Philippines and Singapore refer to 2000, for Brunei to 2001, for Timor-Leste to 2004, for Myanmar and Vietnam to 2007, for Cambodia to 2008. Latest data for Philippines refer to 2007, and for Timor-Leste and Vietnam to 2009. Data for all other years refer to the actual year indicated in the chart

at marriage (based on around 2005 data) with women marrying at 21.7 and men marrying at 24.7, approximately five years younger than in Singapore.

In contrast to the general trend of rising SMAM, several countries in the region have started to show a recent trend in marrying early across genders, such as Vietnam, Cambodia, and Indonesia. Incidentally, men and women from Vietnam and Cambodia are also the youngest to marry in the region. While Vietnam recorded a 1.8-year increase in male SMAM in 40 years from 1970 to 2010, data show that Vietnamese men have been marrying 0.4 years younger in 2010 than in 2005. Its female SMAM however tells a different story with no major fluctuations, recording only a 0.4-year decrease in 40 years.

In Malaysia and Timor-Leste, the consistent trend of marrying later was only observed among women, while men were observed to marry by 0.1 (Malaysia) to 0.6 years (Timor-Leste) earlier within the 2005–2010 period. Malaysia has one of the highest SMAM among women in the region with 25.7 years, almost three years later than Timor-Leste's 23.1 years. Malaysia's rise in female SMAM was also relatively steep, with 3.6 years in a 40-year period which is very close to Singapore's experience. Brunei's female SMAM trend also increased by about three years within 25 years but was stalled from 1995 to 2005, while the rise in SMAM for men has been ongoing for the past 35 years.

3.2 Singlehood

Singlehood rates have been rising in Southeast Asia for the past three decades as measured by the proportion of single women (Fig. 3.2a, b) and men (Fig. 3.3a, b) in their 30s. Some deviations from the trend have been noted, however; such as in Vietnam, Indonesia, and Lao PDR where singlehood rates have declined recently. In Vietnam, the proportion of never-married women within the 2000–2010 period decreased significantly by 4.8 percentage points for the 30–34 age group and by 1.6 percentage points for the 35–39 age group; while in Indonesia, a 1 percentage point decrease for single women in the 30–34 age group was noted, and in Lao PDR, a 0.8 percentage point drop among men in the 35–39 age group. All three countries' female singleness rates in 2010 were below 4%.

Singapore has had the highest rate of singlehood from the 1980s until the turn of the twenty-first century. Looking at Fig. 3.2a, b, Singapore's singlehood rates for women rose from 16.7% in 1980 to 25.1% in 2010 among the 30–34 age group and doubled from 8.5% in 1980 to 17.1% in 2010 for the 35–39 age group. A similar pattern was observed for men where singlehood among the 30–34-year olds increased by 15.6 percentage points to 37.1% and doubled among the 35–39 age group to 20.4%. Singapore's numbers are close to East Asian countries where singlehood rates for men and women range from 37.6% (South Korea) to 49.1% (Japan), which are higher

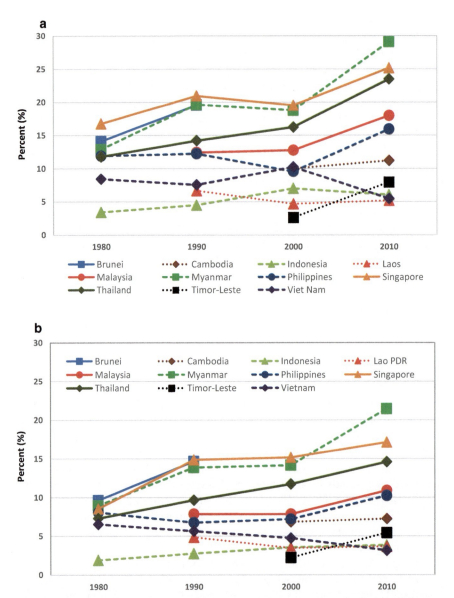

Fig. 3.2 a Singlehood rate among female 30–34-year-olds in Southeast Asia, 1980–2010, **b** singlehood rate among female 35–39-year-olds in Southeast Asia, 1980–2010. *Source* UN World Marriage Data 2015 accessed on 11 October 2016. *Notes* For Brunei, data for 1980 are actually from 1981, for 1990 from 1991; for Cambodia, data for 2000 from 1998, for 2010 from 2008; for Lao PDR, data for 1990 from 1995, for 2010 from 2011; for Malaysia, data for 1990 from 1991; for the Philippines, data for 1990 from 1993; for Timor-Leste, data for 2000 from 2003, for 2010 from 2009; and, for Vietnam, data for 1980 from 1988, for 1990 from 1997. Data for all other years represent the actual year indicated in the chart

3.2 Singlehood

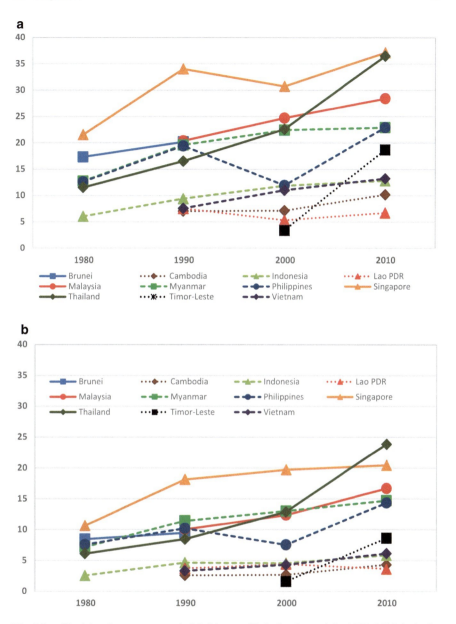

Fig. 3.3 a Singlehood rate among male 30–34-year-olds in Southeast Asia, 1980–2010, **b** singlehood rate among male 35–39-year-olds in Southeast Asia, 1980–2010. *Source* UN World Marriage Data 2015 accessed on 11 October 2016. *Notes* For Brunei, data for 1980 is actually from 1981, for 1990 from 1991; for Cambodia, data for 1990 from 1998, for 2000 from 2004, for 2010 from 1008; for Lao PDR, data for 1990 from 1995, for 2010 from 2011; for Malaysia, data for 1990 from 1991; for Myanmar, data for 1980 from 1983, for 1990 from 1991, for 2010 from 2014; for Philippines, data for 1990 from 1995; for Timor-Leste, data for 2000 from 2003, for 2010 from 2009; and, for Vietnam, data for 1990 from 1980, for 2010 from 2011. Data for all other years refer to the actual year indicated in the chart

than the OECD average of around 15% (Organization for Economic Co-operation & Development, 2011).[1]

A study on singlehood in Singapore postulated that the high rates of singlehood in the country are attributable to a complex set of demographic, economic, and social factors. Commonly cited among these are economic development, increased educational attainment particularly among women causing ideational change, a shift in gender roles, long working hours, and changing social norms characterized by an increasing acceptance of singles and cohabitation (Jones et al., 2012). What then could have caused the temporary stalling in the rise of singlehood rates in the country after 2000? Literature suggest that this can be attributed partly to the growth in the number of permanent residents in the country (Jones et al., 2012, p. 731) and to the government's efforts to encourage marriage and births by providing financial and institutional incentives for those who do so (Jones & Yeung, 2014, p. 1579).

Based on 2010 data, the proportion of single women in Myanmar for the 30–34 and 35–39 age groups are 3.9 and 4.3 percentage points higher than that of Singapore.[2] For men, Singapore still has the highest singlehood rate for the 30–34 age group at 37.1%, which is very close to Thailand at 36.5%. Thailand has the highest singlehood rate for the 35–39 age group at 23.9%, which is 3.5 percentage points higher compared to Singapore's 20.4%.

Rigg (2012, p. 157) elucidated that Myanmar's high level of singlehood, which recently surpassed that of Singapore, is related to Burmese society's social acceptance of singlehood; hence, the pressure to marry is lower compared to other countries in the region. The country's low level of economic development and strong social disapproval of divorce also add to the reluctance of men and women to enter marriage and instead opt for singlehood.

Thailand, Malaysia, the Philippines, Timor-Leste, and Cambodia also show an increase in the proportion of single men and women in their 30s (Abalos, 2014). Over 30 years, the proportion of women never married in Thailand for the 30–34 and 35–39 age groups increased by 11.7 and 7.3 percentage points and by 4 and 2.1 percentage points for the Philippines for the same age group and within the same period. For Malaysia, it increased by 5.5 and 3 percentage points within 20 years. For the same age group but within ten years, Timor-Leste's proportion of single women rose by 5.3 and 3.2 percentage points while Cambodia's rose only by 1.2 and 0.4 percentage points.

Overall, men had a steeper rise in singlehood with rates among the 30–34 and 35–39 year olds in Thailand increasing by 25 and 17.8 percentage points respectively, and in the Philippines by 10.3 and 6.8 percentage points over 30 years. Within two decades, Malaysia's singlehood rates for men aged 30–34 and 35–39 went up by 8 and 6.6 percentage points, while Cambodia's rose by 3.1 and 1.7 percentage points, respectively. Jones pointed out that in Malaysia and Singapore, male singlehood is negatively correlated with education (Rigg, 2012). The fastest rise in singlehood

---

[1] OECD statistics for "single, living alone" includes people aged 20+.

[2] This trend is also mirrored among women in their 40 s where the proportion of single women in Myanmar are higher by 2% to 3.2% than Singapore (data not shown).

3.2 Singlehood

among men in their 30s was in Timor-Leste where a 15.3 and 7 percentage point increase occurred among the same age groups in just a decade between 2000 and 2010 (when data are available for this country). For Brunei, data from 1980–1990 show that the singlehood rate has also increased, but the lack of data after 1990 makes it difficult to track the recent trend of singlehood in the country. These trends have to do with the increase modernization, education, changing gender norms and family ideology discussed in previous chapters.

3.3 Divorce

The UN defines crude divorce rate (CDR) as the number of divorces occurring among the population during the year, per 1000 people estimated at midyear. Figure 3.4 below shows varying divorce trends in Southeast Asia. Data are only available for five countries at different time points.

The fastest increase and highest rate now occurs in Singapore where the CDRs have consistently increased from 0.6 in 1978 to 2 in 2005 followed by a small decline

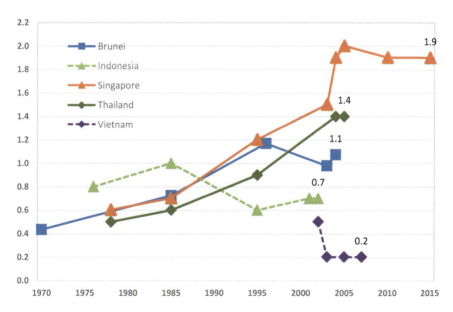

Fig. 3.4 Crude divorce rate in Southeast Asia, 1970–2015. *Source* Data for Brunei (1978, 1985, 1995, 2004, 2005), Thailand (1978, 1985, 1995, 2004, 2005), and Vietnam (2002) from UN Department of Economic and Social Affairs World Marriage Data 2008; for Singapore (1978, 1985, 1995, 2003), Indonesia (1976, 1985, 1995, 2001, 2001), and Vietnam (2003, 2005, 2007) from Dommaraju and Jones (2011); for Singapore (2003–2009) from Singapore Department of Statistics' Key Indicators on Marriages and Divorces, 2004–2009; and for Singapore (2010–2015) from Singapore Department of Statistics' Key Indicators of Marriages and Divorces, 2010–2015. All sources were accessed on 31 October 2016

till 2015. This is comparable with the OECD's average of over two divorces per 1000 people (Organization for Economic Co-operation & Development, 2011). Similarly, Thailand's divorce rates also jumped from 0.5% in 1978 to 1.4% in 2004. However, compared to Singapore where rates further increased from 1.5% in 2003 to 2% in 2005, Thailand's divorce rates stalled at 1.4% in 2004 and 2005. The divorce rates in other countries in this region remain relatively low.

On the contrary, Brunei's divorce rates, while closely resembling Singapore's figures with 0.7% in 1985 and 1.2% in 1996, has dropped to 1% in 2003 with a slight bounce in 2004. Mohammed and Anaman (2003) showed the rising divorce rates caused more women to enter the labour force.

From the middle of the 1970s to the 1980s, Indonesia had the highest rate of divorce in the region; but these numbers dropped almost by half, to 0.6% in 1995 before climbing back up to 0.7% in 2001 and stalling at that level in 2002. The decline in divorce in the 1990s may have been linked to the ideological changes brought by industrialization that veers away from early arranged unions and instead emphasize love, affective bonds, emotional compatibility, and commitment as essential to marriage (Heaton et al., 2001). The reversal of the trend by the turn of the century was proposed to have been a function of an increased exposure to popular media which espouses developmental idealism coupled with the government's recognition and institutionalization of women's rights (Heaton & Cammack, 2011).

Meanwhile, the limited data for Vietnam indicate that divorce rates remain low and have even declined from 0.5% in 2002 to 0.2% in 2003 and stagnated at that level until 2005.

3.4 Consensual Union

While marriage rates in the region are declining and those who marry tend to do so at a later age, statistics also show that a significant proportion of the population is entering into consensual unions or cohabitations. Figure 3.5a, b indicate the percentage of men and women who are in consensual unions in Cambodia, Indonesia, Lao PDR, the Philippines, Thailand, Timor-Leste, and Vietnam at different ages. Data for other countries are not available. It should be noted that data on cohabitation may not be very reliable due to social desirability issues in reporting. Based on available data, the number of women who are in consensual unions is almost four times that of men in such unions. Explanation for this gender discrepancy is unclear. Cohabitation is most notably observed among people in their 20 s and 30 s, peaking at 20–24 for women and 25–29 for men before it goes on a continuous decline until their late 40 s (see also Xenos & Kabamalan, 2007).

Figure 3.5a shows Thailand and the Philippines have the highest percentage of women in consensual unions across all age groups. Thailand's figures range from 13.7% (15–19 age group) to 42.9% (20–24 age group) in 2015 while the Philippines' range from 7.6% (15–19 age group) to 23% (20–24 age group) in 2013. Thailand's numbers are almost double compared to the Philippines and eight times

3.4 Consensual Union

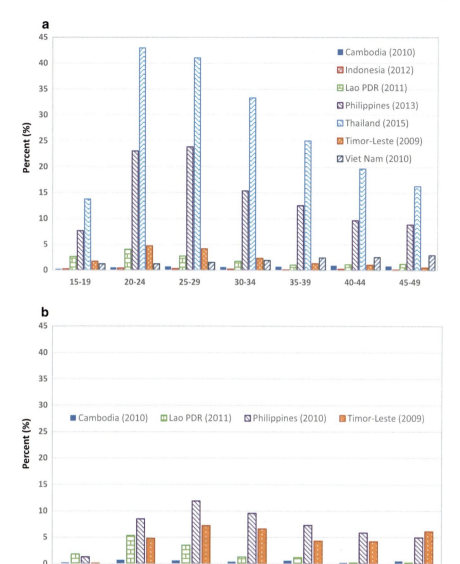

Fig. 3.5 **a** Proportion of women in consensual unions in Southeast Asia, by country and age group, latest available year. *Source* UN World Marriage Data 2015, accessed on 11 October 2016. *Notes* Latest available data for the Philippines refer to 2013, for Lao PDR to 2012, for Cambodia and Vietnam to 2010, for Timor-Leste to 2009, and for Thailand to 2005; **b** proportion of men in consensual unions in Southeast Asia, by country and age group, latest available year. *Source* UN World Marriage Data 2015, accessed on 11 October 2016. *Notes* Latest available data for Lao PDR refer to 2011, for the Philippines and Cambodia to 2010, and for Timor-Leste to 2009

bigger compared to the rest of the countries in the region where the percentage of women in consensual unions does not go beyond 5%. This is a large increase compared to findings in previous research that showed that in 2006, cohabitation only accounted for 2.4% of 18–59-year-old individuals nationally and about 10.2% in Bangkok (Jampaklay & Haseen, 2011).

Other countries that have recorded consensual unions for women were Cambodia, Indonesia, Lao PDR, Timor-Leste, and Vietnam with very low levels ranging from 0.5% to 4%.

For men, Thai data were absent, and the Philippines consistently holds the highest proportion of men in consensual unions particularly among the 25–29 age group at 12%. This is in comparison to the rest of the countries (with available data) where the prevalence of cohabitation is low. Recall that in the Philippines, divorce is prohibited because of the Catholicism tradition there, cohabitation thus may have become an alternative life choice to marriage or after an annulment.

References

Dommaraju, P., & Jones, G. (2011). Divorce trends in Asia. *Asian Journal of Social Science, 39*(6), 725–750. https://doi.org/10.1163/156853111X619201

Heaton, T., & Cammack, M. (2011). Explaining the recent upturn in divorce in Indonesia: Developmental idealism and the effect of political change. *Asian Journal of Social Science, 39*(6), 776–796. https://doi.org/10.1163/156853111X619229

Heaton, T. B., Cammack, M., & Young, L. (2001). Why is the divorce rate declining in Indonesia? *Journal of Marriage and Family, 63*(2), 480–490. https://doi.org/10.1111/j.1741-3737.2001.00480.x

Jampaklay, A., & Haseen, F. (2011). Marital unions and unmarried cohabitation in Bangkok, Thailand: Are cohabiters different from singles or married people? *Asian Population Studies, 7*(2), 137–156.

Jones, G. W., Yanxia, Z., & Zhi, P. C. P. (2012). Understanding high levels of singlehood in Singapore. *Journal of Comparative Family Studies, 43*(5), 731–750.

Jones, G. W., & Yeung, W.-J.J. (2014). Marriage in Asia. *Journal of Family Issues, 35*(12), 1567–1583.

Mohammed, S. J., & Anaman, K. A. (2003). Analysis of causality links between aggregate women labour force and the divorce rate in Brunei Darussalam. In *Applied economic analysis in Brunei Darussalam: Evaluation of economic growth and trade, microeconomic efficiency, and analysis of socio-economic problems* (p. 164): Department of Economics, Faculty of Business, Economics, and Policy Studies, Universiti Brunei Darussalam.

Organization for Economic Co-operation and Development. (2011). *Doing better for families*. Retrieved from http://www.oecd.org/social/family/doingbetter

Rigg, J. (2012). *unplanned development: tracking change in Souheast Asia*. Zed Books Ltd.

Open Access This chapter is licensed under the terms of the Creative Commons Attribution 4.0 International License (http://creativecommons.org/licenses/by/4.0/), which permits use, sharing, adaptation, distribution and reproduction in any medium or format, as long as you give appropriate credit to the original author(s) and the source, provide a link to the Creative Commons license and indicate if changes were made.

The images or other third party material in this chapter are included in the chapter's Creative Commons license, unless indicated otherwise in a credit line to the material. If material is not included in the chapter's Creative Commons license and your intended use is not permitted by statutory regulation or exceeds the permitted use, you will need to obtain permission directly from the copyright holder.

Chapter 4
Fertility

4.1 Total Fertility Rate (TFR)

The total fertility rate (TFR) refers to the number of children that would be borne to a woman if she was to live to the end of her childbearing years and bear children in accordance with age-specific fertility rates of the specified year.

Figure 4.1a, b depict TFRs for SEA countries as of 2014. "Low-fertility countries" are defined as those with TFRs below the population replacement rate of 2.1, while "high-fertility countries" are those with TFRs above 2.1.

Most SEA countries have been experiencing steady declines in TFRs, reflecting a global trend in falling TFR (Lippman & Wilcox, 2015). In 1960, many SEA countries had TFRs around 5–7 but they have all dropped to below 3.0 by 2014, except Timor-Leste. The TFRs for Brunei, Malaysia, and Vietnam have fallen below the population replacement rate of 2.1 since the early 2000s, while Singapore's TFR fell below replacement level since 1975 and Thailand's TFR reached replacement around 1990. Singapore and Thailand's TFR remains the lowest in the region at 1.25 and 1.51 in 2014. The fertility decline in these countries can be attributed to several factors: (1) rising costs of childbearing, be it financial expenses and/or opportunity costs borne by women with interrupted career development; (2) growing societal pressure for women to ensure their children "succeed" in life via "intensive parenting"; and (3) "work–life balance" issues for mothers juggling work and household demands and responsibilities (Jones, 2013, p. 13). In Thailand, the decline in fertility arose from the success of the Thai government's policies in the 1970s encouraging voluntary family planning, with Buddhist values and monks employed to promote women's reproductive autonomy via supporting the use of contraception (Rigg, 2012).

By contrast, Singapore's TFR experienced a brief incline from 1.61 in 1985 to 1.87 in 1990 but fell again to 1.71 in 1995 and has steadily declined ever since. The country has been ranked by the UN as 4th out of the top 10 lowest fertility countries or areas in the world for 2010–2015, with the first 3 being Taiwan, Macao, and Hong Kong (United Nations, 2015, p. 7). Frequently reported struggles of balancing work and family due to limited workplace flexibility, alongside financial constraints,

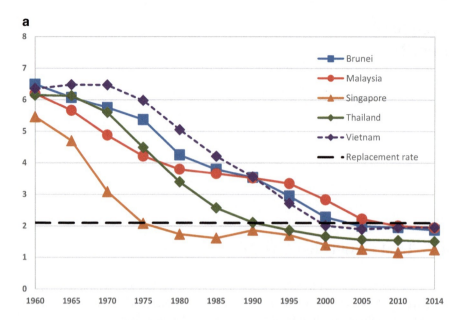

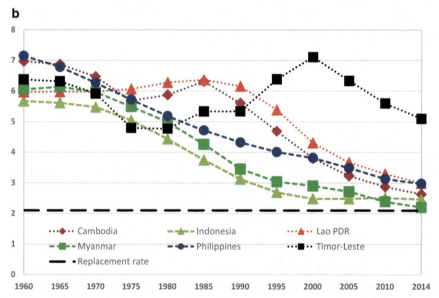

Fig. 4.1 **a** TFR of low-fertility countries in Souheast Asia, 2014, **b** TFR of high-fertility countries in Southeast Asia, 2014. *Source* World Bank database on Health Nutrition and Population Statistics accessed on 25 October 2016. Data for Singapore (2000) sourced from UN Population Division (UNPD) World Fertility Data 2015 accessed on 2 November 2016

and the desire to pursue other forms of fulfilment in life have made Singaporean women more reluctant to have children (Call et al., 2008; Yeung & Hu, 2018). While Singapore's latest TFR has experienced a slow increase from 1.15 in 2010 to 1.25 in 2014, its overall TFR since the mid-1970s has remained very low and is unlikely to increase dramatically within the next decade barring immigration given the size of citizen childbearing-age women will start to shrink and the increasing singleness and permanent childlessness rates in the country.

Despite experiencing overall falls in TFRs, the majority of SEA countries still have relatively high-fertility rates, particularly Cambodia, Lao PDR, and Timor-Leste. The TFRs for these three countries experienced decades of increase before beginning to decline. These drops in fertility resulted from family planning policies in these countries, alongside other factors such as trauma experienced during the Khmer Rouge years in Cambodia, and the small population size and large land resources in Lao PDR (Jones, 2013, p. 30). The Philippines did not experience such drastic changes to its TFR, having undergone a gradual decline since the 1960s with its TFR remained comparatively high at 2.98 in 2014 due to the influence of Catholicism that restricts the use of contraceptives. The TFR in Myanmar reached 2.1 in 2014.

From 1980 to 2014, Timor-Leste experienced the steepest fluctuations in TFR in the region. Its TFR rose sharply from 5.3 in 1990 to 7.11 in 2000 representing a post-war baby boom. Subsequently, TFR fell to 5.10 in 2014. The high-fertility rates in Timor-Leste are related to the country's low socioeconomic development as shown earlier in its low GDP per capita, high poverty rate, low education, and low FLFP level. In 2010, fertility rates remained highest among Timorese women living in poverty, in rural areas, and/or with lower levels of education but have been declining over time among those with higher socioeconomic status due to increased use of, and access to, modern contraception (Bank, 2011). Another reason for Timor-Leste's high-fertility rate has to do with its culture. The 2003 Timor-Leste Demographic and Health Survey (DHS) showed that the majority of Timorese women desired high numbers of children—half the women who had reached the end of their reproductive years in 2003 having given birth to 5.9 children, of whom 4.9 were still alive, wanted more children. This can be seen in the significantly higher number of ideal children shown in Fig. 4.9 in a later section.

4.2 Mean Age at Childbearing (MAC)

The mean age at childbearing (MAC) refers to the mean age of mothers at the birth of their children if women were subject throughout their lives to the age-specific fertility rates observed in a given year. Note that the calculation of MAC only includes women who have children. Figure 4.2a, b illustrate the MAC in Southeast Asia from 1960 to 2010. The mean age of mothers at the birth of their children is shown both for all births and also for first births only.

Four countries have had the MCA at 30 or later since 2000—Malaysia, Myanmar, Singapore, and Timor-Leste. Echoing the shift towards postponement of first birth in

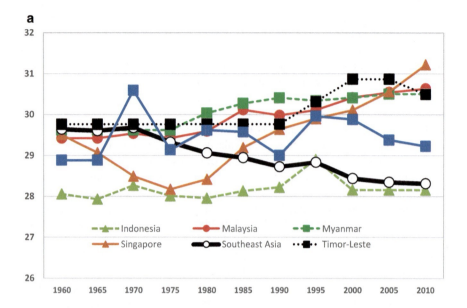

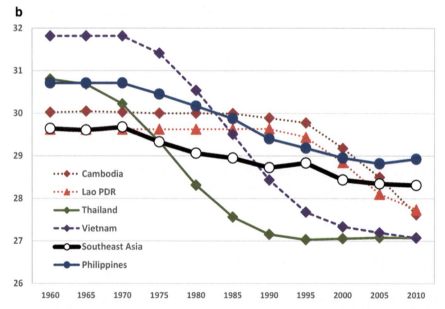

Fig. 4.2 a SEA countries with increasing, or little change in, MAC (as of 2010–2015), **b** SEA countries with decreasing MAC (as of 2010–2015). *Source* Accessed on 23 November 2016. *Notes* Each label in the y-axis represents a 5-year period, e.g. "1960" refers to the period between 1960 and 1965. The data refer to five-year periods running from 1 July to 30 June of the initial and final years

most OECD countries, and following the success of anti-natalist policies to control population growth from the mid-1960s (Call et al., 2008), the MAC in Singapore has been continuously increasing from 28.2 in 1975–1980, to 31.2 in 2010–2015. While Malaysia's MAC remained at a plateau (around 29) from the 1960s to the 1980s, by 1995–2000, the MAC had risen above 30 and has continued to hover around that increased range of 0.5. Myanmar's MAC has been around 30 since the 1980s, from 30.0 in 1980–1985 to 30.5 in 2010–2015. Malaysia and Myanmar's increasing MAC among women reflects similar trends of rapidly rising SMAM, at 25.7 and 26.1 years, respectively, as of 2010 (see Fig. 2.12a).

Although a shift towards delayed childbearing has been observed in many OECD countries, Fig. 4.2b reveals that women in almost half of Southeast Asia are increasingly giving birth at a younger age. Since the 1970s, the MAC in Thailand and Vietnam has decreased exponentially—from 30.2 and 31.8, respectively, in 1970–1975, to 27.1 for both countries in 2010–2015—the lowest in the region. For Cambodia and Lao PDR, the decline in MAC began later between the late 1980s and early 1990s, before falling rapidly across the 1990s to 2010s. Currently, their MAC stands at 27.6 for Cambodia and 27.7 for Lao PDR. These falling rates for MAC correspond with increasing levels of adolescent fertility in said countries, to be described later in Sect. 4.4. Timor-Leste's MAC increased from the early 1990s to the 2000s but the number has recently started decreasing since 2000.

The exception to these trends of increasing or decreasing MAC is Indonesia. Its numbers have remained relatively unchanged across the past 40 years, from 28.3 in 1970–1975 to 28.2 in 2010–2015.

4.3 Age-Specific Fertility Rates (ASFR)

Age-specific fertility rates (ASFR) refer to the number of births to women in a particular age group, divided by the number of women in that age group. Figure 4.3a, b show the latest age-specific fertility rates between 2010 and 2015, categorized based on countries' latest TFR.

While a global shift in delayed childbearing has been reported around the world, most women in SEA continue to give birth in their peak fertility periods between their early to late 20 s. The exception to this trend is Malaysia, Myanmar, and Singapore, where more women appear to be giving birth between their late 20 s and early 30 s. In Malaysia and Myanmar, current fertility rates among 25–29 and 30–34-year olds are the highest among all age groups. Current fertility rates among Malaysian women aged 25–29 are more than double the rates of 20–24-year olds. In Singapore, the current fertility rate of 30–34-year olds is the highest among all age groups and the current fertility rate among 25–29-year-old women is triple that for 20–24-year olds.

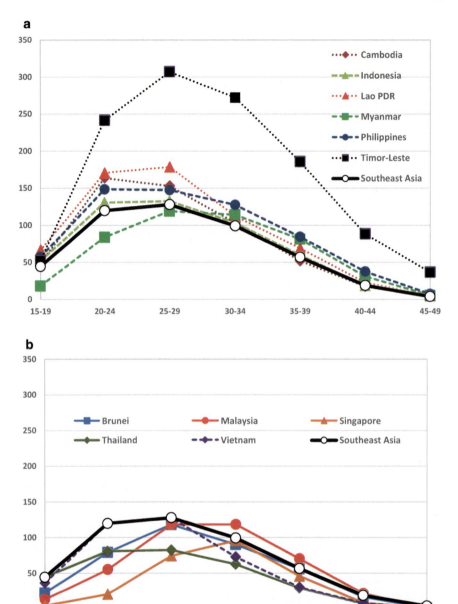

Fig. 4.3 **a** ASFRs in high-fertility countries (as of 2010–2015), by age group, **b** ASFRs in low-fertility countries (as of 2010–2015), by age group. *Source* UNPD World Population Prospects, the 2015 Revision accessed on 23 November 2016

4.3 Age-Specific Fertility Rates (ASFR)

Figure 4.4 shows the ASFRs by five-year age groups for 1970–1975, 1990–1995, and 2010–2015. The changes are more on the levels of fertility rather than the shape of the age-specific curves. In almost all SEA countries, current fertility rates among 20–24, 25–29, and 30–34-year-old women are much lower than they were in 1970. Much of the decline in births among women in their 20s occurred between 1970 and 1990. In Cambodia, Lao PDR, and Malaysia, the fertility rates for women fell at a drastic pace from the 1990s onwards. Conversely, age-specific fertility patterns in Timor-Leste have remained relatively stable from the 1970s to 2010s. In Indonesia,

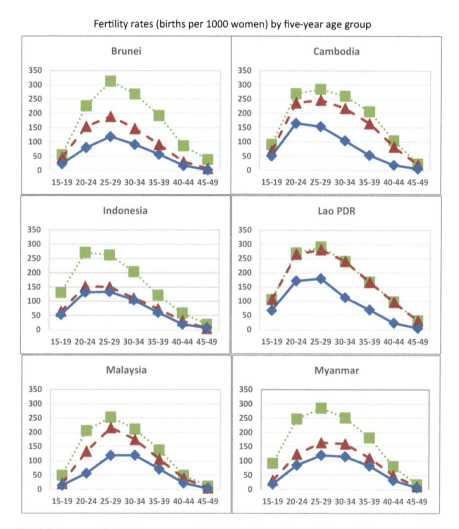

Fig. 4.4 Age-specific fertility rates in 1970–1975, 1990–1995, and 2010–2015. *Source* UNPD World Population Prospects, the 2015 Revision accessed on 23 November 2016

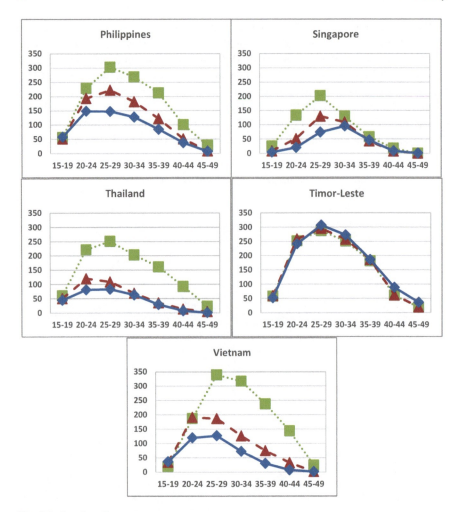

Fig. 4.4 (continued)

Thailand, and Vietnam, the change in age-specific fertility rates is relatively small between the 1990s and 2010s.

4.4 Adolescent Fertility Rates

Adolescent fertility rates refer to births per 1000 women aged 15–19 years old in the population. Figure 4.5 illustrates the general trend in adolescent fertility rates across Southeast Asia.

We observe dramatic declines in adolescent fertility rates in Indonesia, Myanmar, Malaysia, and Singapore since the late 1960s. This decline was manifested two decades later in Lao PDR, even if its adolescent fertility rate remains the highest at 64.5 in 2014. Cambodia saw a similar decline since the 1980s. Indonesia experienced an impressive decline from 143 in 1960 to 48 in 2014. In Timor-Leste, the adolescent fertility rate rose from 51.8 in 1980 to 70.8 in 2000 reflecting the post-war baby boom and lack of contraceptives in the country. Even though the rate started to decline after 2000, it remains relatively high at 47.7 in 2014.

The sharpest decline in Singapore occurred between 1960 and 1980. The country has the lowest adolescent fertility rates in the region, which stood at 3.8 in 2014. It is also ranked 6th out of the top 10 countries or areas with the lowest adolescent birth rates (United Nations, 2015, p. 11).

Despite a decrease in overall adolescent fertility rates across Southeast Asia, several countries are experiencing a surprising increase in current adolescent fertility rates. In Vietnam, the adolescent fertility rate has more than doubled from 1975 (18.9) to 2014 (38.1). According to Nguyen et al. (2016), the rise in teenage pregnancy in Vietnam can be attributed to more teenagers having sex outside of marriage and at earlier ages, alongside rising occurrences of drug addiction, delinquency, and high-risk sexual behaviour that could potentially lead to HIV/AIDS (p. 5). These

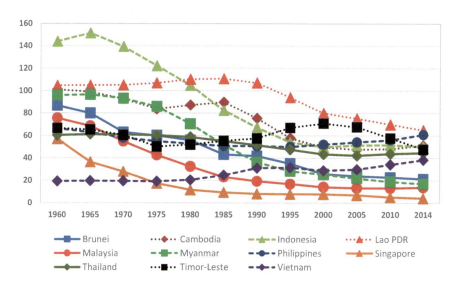

Fig. 4.5 Adolescent fertility rates (births per 1000 women aged 15–19) in Southeast Asia, 1960–2015. *Source* World Bank database on Gender Statistics accessed on 26 October 2016

teenagers tend to live in rural, economically disadvantaged areas, and tend to have lower levels of education, no access to the Internet and/or sex education at school, depressive symptoms, and live in families with a history of domestic violence (p. 11). Cultural norms may also play a significant role, such as the normative expectations of traditional ethnic minorities living in the mountains who may see little issue with marriage and pregnancy at a younger age, and increasing acceptance of premarital sex due to teenagers' consumption of Western movies, news, music, and social media propagating Western sexual norms, for those who have access to it (p. 12).

While the number in the Philippines fell from 54.8 in 1975 to 49.8 in 1995, teenage pregnancy has steadily risen to 60.8 in 2014, marking an increase of more than 22% in the last 20 years or so. Its adolescent fertility rate is also currently the second highest in the region, after Lao PDR, which is experiencing a decline in its numbers. Although early childbearing in both the Philippines and Vietnam is more prominent among those with elementary level schooling, those in rural areas, and those with poorer socioeconomic status, Natividad (2014) highlighted that recent upsurges in early childbearing in the Philippines are especially pronounced among those in urban areas (62.5% increase from 1993 to 2008) and those with a college education (290% increase from 1993 to 2008). She suggested that the rising proportion of urban, better educated teenage mothers from the middle to highest socioeconomic groups may have stemmed from widespread premarital sexual activity at an early age—a finding supported by the country's high prevalence of consensual unions, which range from 7.6% for 15–19-year olds to 23% for 20–24-year olds (see Fig. 3.4a).

The numbers for Cambodia and Thailand reached their lowest point in 2005, before slowly increasing by about 5.5–7.5% in 2014. Despite being one of the SEA countries with the lowest adolescent fertility rates, Malaysia's adolescent fertility rate has recently increased to 13.4 in 2014.

4.5 Childlessness

Figure 4.6 illustrates available data on childlessness as reported among women aged 40–44 years old.

Singapore stands out as the only country with exponential growth in childlessness among women aged 40–44—from 6.9% in 2000 to 23.2% in 2010, signifying a 337% increase within a decade. This coheres with findings from the UNPD which revealed that Singapore has the highest level of childlessness among women aged 40–44 in low-fertility countries across the world (United Nations, 2014, p. 13). Although the numbers do not distinguish involuntary from voluntary childlessness, a 2008 study highlighting that Singaporean women aged 40–45 report the lowest mean ideal number of children (2.3) among their age and gender cohorts may point towards the prevalence of the latter (Call et al., 2008, p. 101).

4.5 Childlessness

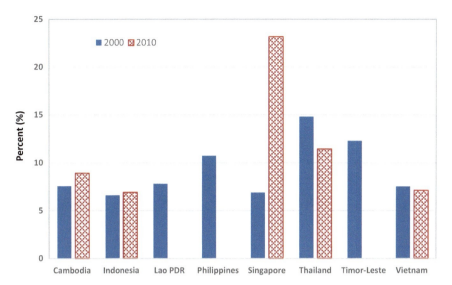

Fig. 4.6 Childlessness among women aged 40–44, years 2000, 2010. *Source* UNSD Demographic Statistics accessed on 2 November 2016. *Notes* (a) 2000 data for Lao PDR refer to 1995, for Cambodia to 1998, for Vietnam to 1999, and for Timor-Leste to 2004. 2010 data for Cambodia refer to 2008, and for Vietnam to 2009. Data for all other years refer to the actual year indicated in the chart; (b) Data for Thailand (2000) and Vietnam (2010) is based on provisional figures from census data; (c) No available data for Brunei, Lao PDR (2010), Malaysia, Myanmar, the Philippines (2010), and Timor-Leste (2010)

Thailand has the second-highest childlessness rate at 11.4% in 2010. Interestingly, the percentage of childless women within the same age group has decreased from 14.8% in 2000 to 11.4% by 2010. Thus, despite the country's falling TFR, women continue to give birth to children, a finding which is also supported by their decreasing mean age of childbearing. In all other countries, the prevalence is lower than 10%. The percentage of childless women within the 40–44 years old-age group in Cambodia, Indonesia, and Vietnam has remained relatively unchanged from 2000 to 2010.

Figure 4.7 depicts "definitive childlessness" as reported among women aged 45–49, where they have reached the end of their reproductive period. Definitive childlessness mirrors the trends of childlessness for women aged 40–44 as discussed in the preceding section. Cambodia, Indonesia, and Vietnam's definitive childlessness have remained relatively unchanged from 2000 to 2010, while in Thailand, the percentages have fallen from 13.63% in 2000 to 10.17% in 2010. Again, Singapore's rate of childless women aged 45–49 has increased rapidly within the same period to 20%.

Figure 4.8a shows a different view of the childlessness rate—the proportion of childlessness among women across birth cohorts as recorded in 2000. Data were only available for Cambodia, Singapore, Thailand, and Timor-Leste. Childlessness rates in Thailand increased across the different birth cohorts from 5% among the 1926 birth cohort to 15% among the 1956 birth cohort. In Singapore, there was an initial decline in childlessness among those born in 1921 but rose slightly for cohorts

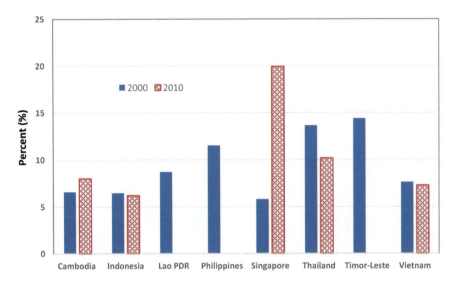

Fig. 4.7 Definitive childlessness among women in Southeast Asia aged 45–49 (2000, 2010). *Source* UNSD Demographic Statistics accessed on 2 November 2016. *Notes* (a) 2000 data for Lao PDR refer to 1995, for Cambodia to 1998, for Vietnam to 1999, and for Timor-Leste to 2004. 2010 data for Cambodia refer to 2008, and for Vietnam to 2009. Data for all other years refer to the actual year indicated in the chart; (b) Data for Thailand (2000) and Vietnam (2010) is based on provisional figures from census data; (c) No available data for Brunei, Lao PDR (2010), Malaysia, Myanmar, the Philippines (2010), and Timor-Leste (2010)

born in the early 1930s and continue to increase to 6.9% for the 1956 cohort. Timor-Leste was an exception to this trend, with childlessness being the highest within Southeast Asia at 36.1% among cohorts born in the 1920s, and sharply decreasing among cohorts born in later periods to 12% among the cohort born in 1956. This may be due to a prevalent "post-genocidal" psychology wherein many believe that they have to replace lost family members with more children (Saikia, Dasvarma, & Wells-Brown, 2009).

In comparison, Fig. 4.8b shows how the proportion of childlessness among women differs across countries and age cohorts, as recorded in 2010. The chart focuses on Indonesia, Singapore, and Thailand as data were only available for these countries. For Singapore and Thailand, there is an increase among younger cohorts. The increase is particularly sharp for Singapore women born after 1941, from 9% to 23.2% among women born in 1966. Note that by 2010, the year of the report, the youngest cohort (born in 1966) in Fig. 4.8b would have been 44 years old, nearing the end of the conventional childbearing age. With almost one in four women at this age remained childless, this is among the highest childless rates observed in the world. The reverse trend is observed in Indonesia where the childlessness rate has declined across birth cohorts to 6.9% among women born in 1966.

4.5 Childlessness

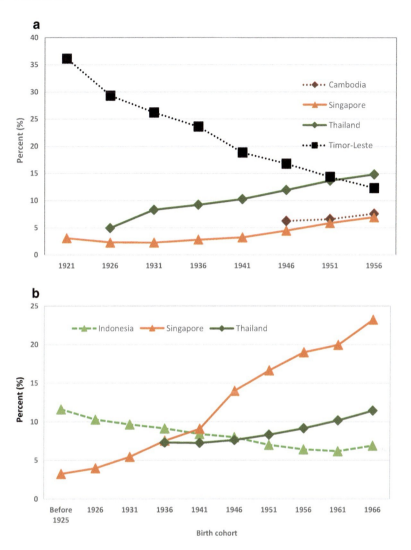

Fig. 4.8 a Childless women per birth cohort, recorded in 2000. *Source* UNSD Demographic Statistics accessed on 2 November 2016. *Notes* (a) Years indicated in the x-axis refer to those born within five years from the indicated year, e.g. 1926 refers to the cohort of women born between 1926 and 1930; (b) Data for Cambodia refer to 1998, for Timor-Leste to 2004; (c) Data for Thailand are based on provisional figures from census data; (d) Those under 1946 birth cohort in Cambodia refer to women listed as aged 50+ in the UNSD Demographic Statistics report; (e) Those under 1921 birth cohorts in Singapore and Timor-Leste refer to women listed as aged 75+ in the UNSD Demographic Statistics report. **b** Childless women per cohort in 2010. *Source* UNSD Demographic Statistics accessed on 2 November 2016. *Notes* (a) Years indicated in the x-axis refer to those born within five years from the indicated year, e.g. 1926 refers to the cohort of women born between 1926 and 1930; (b) Those under the 1936 birth cohort in Thailand refer to women listed as aged 70+ in the UNSD Demographic Statistics report

4.6 Ideal and Actual Fertility Rates

The ideal fertility rate is based on the wanted fertility rate, which is an estimate of what the total fertility rate would be if all unwanted births were avoided. The actual fertility rate is based on the total fertility rate recorded in the same year when the ideal numbers of children were recorded.

Figure 4.9 compares the mean average personal ideal number of children with the actual fertility rate for Cambodia, Indonesia, the Philippines, Timor-Leste, and Vietnam.

Based on the chart, we can see how observed total fertility rates are between 2 and 3 and they tend to be higher than ideal fertility rates (except for Singapore), a pattern that drastically contrasts with what has been observed in OECD countries. The difference between ideal and actual fertility rates tend to be around 0.2 to 0.5 child except for the Philippines where the differences were 1.1 and 0.8 children in 2000 and 2014 respectively which may reflect the restriction on contraceptives (See also David & Atun, 2014).

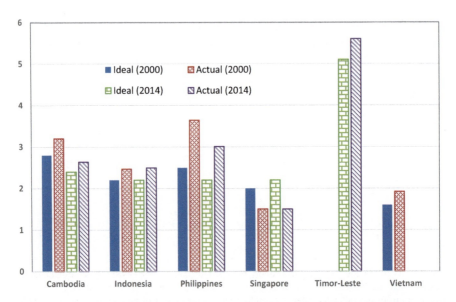

Fig. 4.9 Ideal and actual fertility rates, 2000, 2014. *Source* World Bank Gender Statistics accessed on 26 October 2016 except for Singapore; data for Singapore from National Population and Talent Division (NPTD), Marriage and Population Survey 2012 accessed on 5 December 2016. *Notes* (a) 2000 data for Vietnam refer to 2002, for Indonesia and Philippines to 2003, for Singapore to 2004, and for Cambodia to 2005. 2014 data for Timor-Leste refer to 2010, for Indonesia and Singapore to 2012, and for the Philippines to 2013. Data for all other years refer to the actual year indicated in the chart; (b) Data not available for Brunei, Lao PDR, Malaysia, Myanmar, Thailand, Timor-Leste (2000) and Vietnam (2014)

Overall, the ideal number of children in Timor-Leste is much higher than the numbers for other SEA countries—5.1 in 2000. This may be due to cultural beliefs among men in Timor-Leste where big families are desired. There is also the existence of a widespread norm that women need to "compensate" their bride price by bearing many children (Saikia et al., 2009). Additionally, the tradition of "assigning" children to the *uma lisan* or "Traditional/Cultural House" makes it culturally desirable for families to have more children to ensure the families' ability to carry on their culture through future generations (Saikia et al., 2009). Accordingly, despite undergoing its first demographic transition with declining fertility rates, it is predicted that Timor-Leste will not experience drastic fertility decline due to the prevalent cultural preference for more children (Hosgelen & Saikia, 2016, p. 249).

Singapore is an outlier among SEA countries in that its actual observed total fertility rates were lower than the ideal fertility rates. A survey in 2012 shows that 80% of singles and 84% of married respondents were reported to desire two or more children, and both male and female respondents expressed an average ideal of 2.2 children (National Population & Talent Division, 2013), notably higher than the actual fertility rates in 2000 (1.4) and 2010 (1.15). Despite Singapore's low-fertility levels, ideal family sizes have more or less remained similar from 2004 to 2012 (NPTD, 2013). With 80% of single female respondents desiring to be working mothers, and 77% of married female respondents desiring employment after having a child (NPTD, 2013), it is evident that issues related to "work–life balance", such as job opportunity and family–work conflict, high cost and social pressure noted earlier remain significant constraints for Singaporeans to achieve their childbearing aspiration.

References

Bank, W. (2011). *Reproductive health at a glance—Timor-Leste.* Retrieved from Washington, DC http://siteresources.worldbank.org/INTPRH/Resources/376374-1282255445143/TimorLeste52411web.pdf

Call, L. L., Sheffield, R., Trail, E., Yoshida, K., & Hill, E. J. (2008). Singapore's fertility: Exploring the influence of the work-family interface. *International Journal of Sociology of the Family, 34*(1), 91–113.

Hosgelen, M., & Saikia, U. (2016). Timor-Leste's demographic challenges for environment, peace and nation-building. *Asia Pacific Viewpoint, 57*(2), 244–262. https://doi.org/10.1111/apv.12117

Jones, G. (2013). The population of Southeast Asia. *Asia Research Institute Working Paper Series, 196*, 1–39.

Lippman, L. H., & Wilcox, W. B. (2015). *World family map 2015: Mapping family change and child well-being outcomes.* Retrieved from http://www.childtrends.org/wp-content/uploads/2015/09/2015-39WorldFamilyMap2015.pdf

National Population and Talent Division. (2013). *Marriage and parenthood study 2012.* Retrieved from Singapore http://www.nptd.gov.sg/portals/0/news/mp-study-2012-press-release.pdf

Natividad, J. (2014). Teenage pregnancy in the Philippines: Trends, correlates and data sources. *Journal of the ASEAN Federation of Endocrine Societies, 28*(1).

Nguyen, H., Shiu, C., & Farber, N. (2016). Prevalence and factors associated with teen pregnancy in Vietnam: Results from two national surveys. *Societies, 6*(2), 17.

Rigg, J. (2012). *Unplanned development: Tracking change in Souheast Asia*. Zed Books Ltd.

Saikia, U., Dasvarma, G. L., & Wells-Brown, T. (2009). *The world's highest fertility in Asia's newest nation: an investigation into reproductive behaviour of women in Timor-Leste*. Paper presented at the XXVI IUSSP International Population Conference, Morocco. http://iussp2009.princeton.edu/papers/90513

United Nations. (2014). *World fertility report 2013: Fertility at the extremes*. Retrieved from New York http://www.un.org/en/development/desa/population/publications/pdf/fertility/worldFertilityReport2013.pdf

United Nations. (2015). *World fertility patterns 2015*. Retrieved from New York http://www.un.org/en/development/desa/population/publications/pdf/fertility/world-fertility-patterns-2015.pdf

Yeung, W.-J. J., & Hu, S. (2018). *Family and population changes in Singapore: A unique case in global F.*

Open Access This chapter is licensed under the terms of the Creative Commons Attribution 4.0 International License (http://creativecommons.org/licenses/by/4.0/), which permits use, sharing, adaptation, distribution and reproduction in any medium or format, as long as you give appropriate credit to the original author(s) and the source, provide a link to the Creative Commons license and indicate if changes were made.

The images or other third party material in this chapter are included in the chapter's Creative Commons license, unless indicated otherwise in a credit line to the material. If material is not included in the chapter's Creative Commons license and your intended use is not permitted by statutory regulation or exceeds the permitted use, you will need to obtain permission directly from the copyright holder.

Chapter 5
Household Structures

5.1 Average Household Size in Southeast Asia, 1980–2010

The average household size is calculated as the mean average number of people per household by household type.

Figure 5.1 indicates how the average household size has generally declined in Southeast Asia over the past three decades from 1980 to 2010. Lao PDR has the largest average household size at 5.9 persons in 2005 which declined only slightly from 6.0 in 1995. All other SEA countries have had a household size of about 5 in 1980, and have experienced a decline over the decades at varying trajectories. Factors affecting this phenomenon include the overall marriage and fertility decline in the region (Fig. 4.1a, b) and increased migration in the region. Singapore has the smallest household size at 3.5 persons in 2010, with Indonesia close behind at 3.9 persons. Interestingly, household size in Thailand appears to decrease at a faster rate than Singapore from 5.1 to 4.9 in 1980 respectively to 3.7 persons (for both countries) in 2000. The household size in Vietnam has also been declining rapidly from about 4.8 in 1985 to below 3.8 in 2005. The Philippines, Myanmar, and Cambodia still have a household size of about 5 in the early 2000s. These trends also suggest that intergenerational co-resident households are still prevalent in Southeast Asia (Esteve & Liu, 2014).

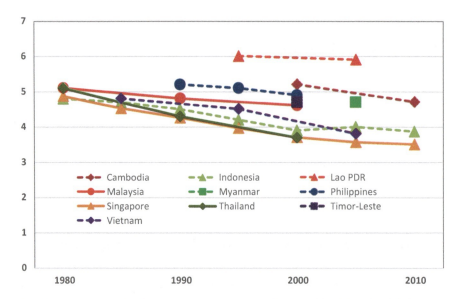

Fig. 5.1 Average household size in Southeast Asia, 1980–2010. *Source* Various Statistical Offices, IPUMS-international, Demographic Health Surveys and United Nations data, as cited from Esteve and Liu (2014, p. 34). Data for Singapore from Population in Brief 2016, p. 124. *Note* No information for Brunei

5.2 Household Types in Southeast Asia, 1970–2010

5.2.1 Nuclear Households with Children

Nuclear family households, or households composed of a couple with children, are still the most common form of household in Southeast Asia. However, consistent with the general trend of decreasing fertility rates in the region, the proportion of nuclear families has been increasing since the 1970s. Large drops in the number of married couples with children were observed in Singapore where the proportion dropped from 66.5% in 1990 to 56.0% in 2010, in Thailand from 50.6% in 1980 to 43.7% in 2000, and in Indonesia from 59.6% in 2000 to 53.0% in 2010 (Fig. 5.2). These recent declines indicate the increase in other types of family structure. Studies have shown that the nuclear family system in Java dates back to at least the nineteenth century and to as early as the fifteenth century in Vietnam (Schrö der-Butterfill, 2004; Schrö der-Butterfill & Marianti, 2006) .

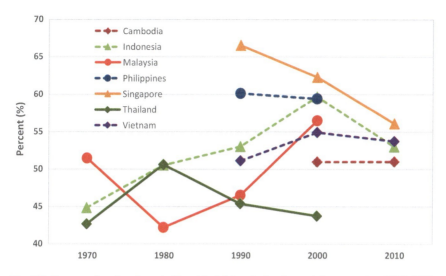

Fig. 5.2 Percent of nuclear households with children in Southeast Asian countries, 1970–2010. *Source* IPUMS-international Version 6.4. Data for Singapore from Population in Brief 2016, pp. 128–129. *Notes* (a) No information available for Brunei, Lao PDR, Myanmar, and Timor-Leste. (b) Singapore data refer to married couples only, no cohabitation

5.2.2 Number of Nuclear Households Without Children Are Rising

In comparison with the idealized nuclear family households which includes children, there appears to be a low incidence of childless nuclear households although we see a gradually rising trend of married or cohabiting households with no children in the region from 1970 to 2010. From about 1.5–2.9% in the 1970s, households with married or cohabiting couples with no children range around 2–5% in 2010 (Fig. 5.3). Singapore is, again, an exception where the proportion of married or cohabiting couples with no children has been high, from 8.4% in 1990 to 13.7% in 2010, or almost three to six times higher than the figures in other SEA countries.

Recent trends in Vietnam and Thailand also show a rapid increase in this type of household. In Vietnam, households of childless married/cohabiting couples rose by 135% in ten years while Thailand's numbers rose by 176% in twenty years.

Other countries in the region showed a slow and gradual increase over the past years such as the Philippines where households of childless couples only rose by 25.3% in ten years, in Malaysia by 33.2% over twenty years, and in Cambodia where households of childless couples increased by 36.1% in ten years. Indonesia also showed an increasing trend from 1970 to 2000 though a gradual reversal from 2000 to 2010.

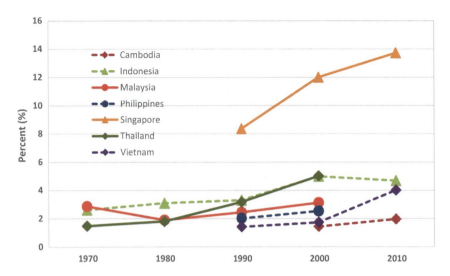

Fig. 5.3 % of childless nuclear households in Southeast Asia, 1970–2010. *Source* IPUMS-international Version 6.4. Data for Singapore from Population in Brief 2016, pp. 128–129. *Notes* (a) Data not available for Brunei, Lao PDR, Myanmar, and Timor-Leste. (b) Singapore data refer to married couples only, no cohabitation

5.2.3 No Clear Trend for Extended Family Households

Next to nuclear family households, extended family households are also prevalent in Southeast Asia. Extended family households are households that are composed of a nuclear family and another person/s who is/are related to either the husband or the wife. An example would be three-generation households where at least one grandparent resides with one of their married children as well as their grandchildren. Figure 5.4 shows that the incidences are highly varied across countries with numbers ranging from 10% in Vietnam to 40% in Thailand in the early 2000s.

The proportion of extended family households has been consistently high in Thailand, and it has been increasing since the 1970s. There has also been a recent rise in extended family households in Cambodia, Indonesia, and Vietnam. From 2000 to 2010, Indonesia and Vietnam's extended family households increased by 4–5%, a much faster movement than Cambodia's 1% increase within the same period.

On the other hand, we could see extended family households declined in Malaysia from 1980 to 2000 by about 7 percentage points. Indonesia saw a decrease since 1990 but a reverse trend since 2000. Figures for the Philippines barely moved in ten years with 26.9% in 1990 and 26.8% in 2000.

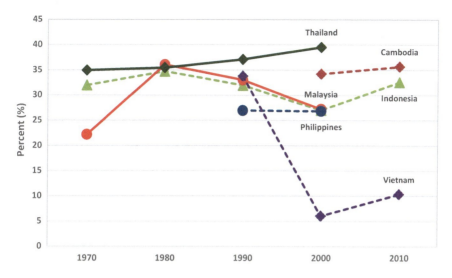

Fig. 5.4 % of extended family households in Southeast Asia, 1970–2010. *Source* IPUMS-international Version 6.4. *Notes* (a) Data not available for Brunei, Lao PDR, Myanmar, Singapore, and Timor-Leste. (b) Year 2000 data for Indonesia are from the year 2005

5.2.4 Decreasing Single-Parent Households

Available data show that single-parent households are not common in Southeast Asia compared to Western societies. Figure 5.5 shows that the prevalence is lower than 10% in all countries, and there is a general decrease in single-parent households (SPH) in this area from 1970–2010. Malaysia in particular experienced a drastic drop in SPH in only a decade, from 9.3% in 1970 to 5.1% in 1980. It continued to drop over the years at a slower rate and had the lowest incidence of SPH among all other Southeast Asian countries in 2000. Other countries which have had rapidly declining SPH rates are Vietnam and Cambodia, at similar rates. In Vietnam, SPH decreased by almost 40% in two decades, from 1990 to 2010. Similarly, the incidence of SPH in Cambodia decreased by almost 20% in only a decade. On the contrary, there appears to be a gradual increase in the rates of such households in Thailand and a marginal increase for the Philippines, from 4.7% in 1970 to 5.6% in 2010, and from 4.3% in 1990 to 4.5% in 2000, respectively.

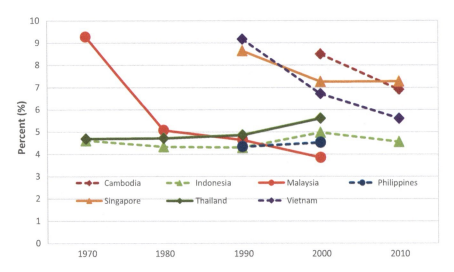

Fig. 5.5 % of single-parent households (SPH) in Southeast Asia, 1970–2010. *Source* IPUMS-international Version 6.4. Data for Singapore from Population in Brief 2016, pp. 128–129. *Notes* Data not available for Brunei, Lao PDR, Myanmar, and Timor-Leste

5.2.5 Drop in the Prevalence of Composite Households

Composite households are households where at least one of the persons living in that household is not related in any way to the head of the family.[1] Figure 5.6 indicates that composite households in the region, which are more common than SPH, have dropped considerably in the last four decades. From having the highest percentage of composite households at 11.0% in 1970, Thailand in 2000 had one of the lowest numbers of such households at around 2% together with Indonesia and Cambodia. Cambodia's numbers slid a bit further to 1.76% in 2010 while Indonesia went slightly up to 2.12% in the same year. Although Malaysia started at around the same level as Indonesia in 1970 before a rapid drop which was slightly cushioned in 1980, its 2000 figures of 3% are still one percentage point higher than Indonesia's.

The Philippines and Vietnam mirrored the overall decline from 1990 to 2000 although at different levels. The Philippines has the highest proportion of composite households in the region based on recent data at 4.9% while Vietnam has the lowest proportion at close to 0%. In the urban Philippines, household sharing for economic and social support is common even among non-relatives (Dommaraju & Tan, 2014) which may contribute to the relatively higher number of composite households in the country.

---

[1] See IPUMS-international Version 6.4 metadata for an exhaustive definition of composite households.

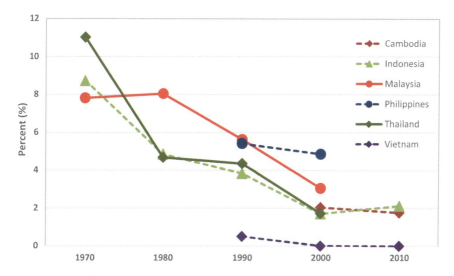

Fig. 5.6 % of composite households in Southeast Asia, 1970–2010. *Source* IPUMS-international Version 6.4. Data for Singapore from Population in Brief 2016, pp. 128–129. *Notes* Data not available for Brunei, Lao PDR, Myanmar, and Timor-Leste

5.2.6 Rising One-Person Households

One-person household (OPH) is a growing global phenomenon that is not yet prevalent in Southeast Asia except in Singapore where OPH rose dramatically from 6% in 1980 to 12% in 2010, as seen in Fig. 5.7, and continued to increase since then. This is about six times higher than the rest of Southeast Asia where OPH in 2010 was around 2.3%. However, this is still lower than economically developed East Asian countries such as Japan, South Korea, and Taiwan where OPH is at 32.4%, 23.9% and 22%, respectively, or in OECD countries (except Mexico) where OPH ranges from 17 to 38% of all households (Yeung & Cheung, 2015, p. 1100). An interview with elderlies living alone in Singapore revealed that living alone was either a product of circumstance or a personal preference, although most have expressed their preference for it after initially being forced by circumstances to live alone (Wong & Verbrugge, 2009, p. 215).

From a very low proportion of 0.85% in 1970, Thailand's OPH has also shown indications of a steep rise since 1990 reaching 2.32% in 2000, overtaking Malaysia and Indonesia which had higher OPH rates in the 1970s to the 1990s. Podhisita and Xenos (2015) observed that high OPH rates are recorded in the Thai urban sector for females, and for both urban and rural among males, suggesting that joining the military or monkhood may play a role in such patterns.

Indonesia, the Philippines, and Vietnam's OPH levels are also rising albeit at a slower rate than Singapore and Thailand.

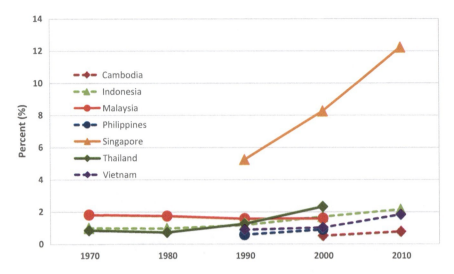

Fig. 5.7 % of one-person households (OPH) in Southeast Asia, 1970–2010. *Source* IPUMS-international Version 6.4. Data for Singapore from Population in Brief 2016, pp. 128–129. *Notes* Data not available for Brunei, Lao PDR, Myanmar, and Timor-Leste

With regard to the demographics of people living alone, Podihista and Xenos (2015) noted that young single people (ages 15–29) are a minority, while the elderly and single account for about 6% in Indonesia (females), to over 20% in Malaysia, the Philippines (males), Thailand (males), and Vietnam (females) (p. 1136). Young adults who live alone in group quarters are common. Despite the large variability of OPH among countries when disaggregated according to gender, age, marital status, and location, the authors noticed that generally, OPH is rising among the young, declines in middle age and surges very high among the elderly. They also argued that while OPH levels are low in the region, they are significant enough to warrant policy considerations.

5.3 Living Arrangements Among Older Adults in Southeast Asia

Considering that Southeast Asia is at the onset of a population ageing trend with Singapore and Thailand paving the way followed by Vietnam and Indonesia, it is important to examine the living arrangements of the elderly.

5.3 Living Arrangements Among Older Adults in Southeast Asia

5.3.1 Living with Their Children or Spouse

Figure 5.8a, b show that the proportion of the elderly living with their children is still predominant in Southeast Asia, with numbers ranging from 50 to 70% of adults in

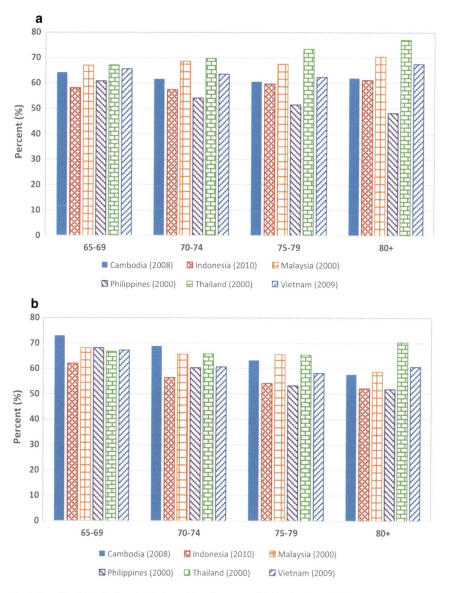

Fig. 5.8 **a** % of elderly females living with at least one child in Southeast Asia, by latest available year, **b** % of elderly males living with at least one child in Southeast Asia, by latest available year. *Source* IPUMS-international Version 6.4

each country under specific age groups. Across countries, Thailand has the highest proportion of the elderly living with their children, especially among elderly females regardless of age group, with the proportion increasing as they age. Malaysia and Indonesia are also following the same trend for females, contrary to the Philippines' inversely proportional movement. For the elderly males, Cambodia has the highest proportion particularly among the 65–69 and 70–74 age groups while Thailand dominates the 80+ age groups. Cambodia's trend shows a decreasing proportion of elderly males living with their children as they age, contrary to Thailand's increasing trend. In Myanmar, about 77% of older adults live with their children (based on 2012 figures) (Knodel & Nguyen, 2015, p. 1967) while in Singapore, about 23% are in three-generation households (based on 2014 figures) (Ministry of Social & Family Development, 2015, p. 7).

Among the Chinese Singaporeans in Singapore, caring for their elderly parents is seen as an epitome of filial piety and hence co-residence with them is a common practice (Voon Chin & Loh, 2008, p. 659). Living with them however is not solely dependent on individual family's preferences but is also influenced by other factors, one of which is the state's housing policies that facilitate co-residence. In most cases, practical and emotional considerations as well as changing cultural and social norms largely affect co-residence choices not only in Singapore but in Thailand and the Philippines as well (Asis et al., 1995; Mehta et al., 1995). Asis et al. (1995) attribute the prevalence of cultural norms about the family's primary role as an institution for elderly caregiving to encouraging co-residence in these countries.

5.3.2 Rise in the Number of Independently Living Older Adults

In this report, older adults who are living independently are categorized into two groups: (1) those who are living solely with their spouse, and (2) those who live on their own.

The next most common living arrangement among the elderly is to live with their spouse. Figure 5.9a, b show that more males are living with their spouses compared to females due to the longer life expectancy of females than males. The percentage of female older adults who are living with their spouses accounts for around 40–50% of the 65–69-year olds, with the numbers decreasing as they age, dropping down to the 10–20% level when they reach their 80s. This number is only about half of the males, where around 80% of the 65–69-year olds live solely with their spouse, with the numbers decreasing as they age, falling to the 50–60% levels in their 80+ years.

At first glance, the percentage of the elderly who are living on their own in Southeast Asia is still not as common as those who live with their children or their spouse, accounting for barely 20% of female elderlies (Fig. 5.10a) and 10% of males (Fig. 5.10b) within the respective countries and age groups. Across countries and

5.3 Living Arrangements Among Older Adults in Southeast Asia 71

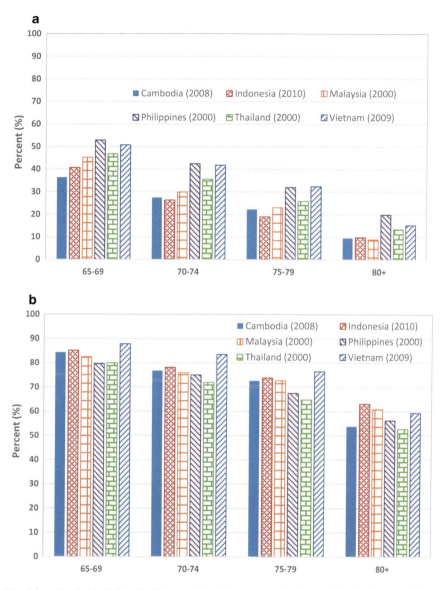

Fig. 5.9 **a** % of elderly females living solely with spouse in Southeast Asia, by latest available year, **b** % of elderly males living solely with spouse in Southeast Asia, by latest year. *Source* IPUMS-international Version 6.4

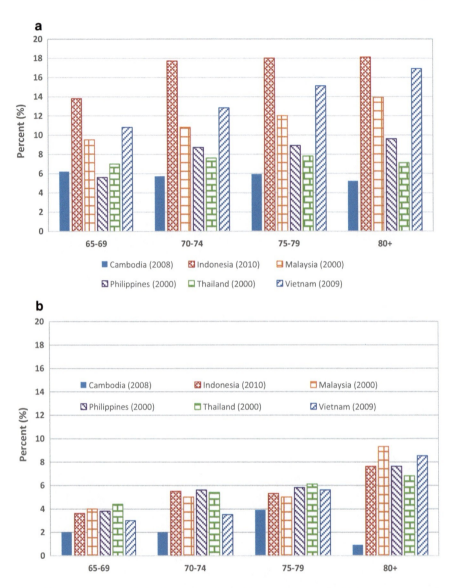

Fig. 5.10 **a** % of female elderly living alone in Southeast Asia, latest available year, **b** % of male elderly living alone in Southeast Asia, latest available year. *Source* IPUMS-international Version 6.4

age groups, Indonesia has the highest proportion of female elderly living alone (14–18%), followed by Vietnam (10.8–16.9%), and Malaysia (9.5–13.9%). Less than 8% of female elderlies in the 65–69, 70–74, 75–79, and 80+ age groups are living alone in Cambodia, the Philippines, and Thailand.

Compared with women, Fig. 5.10b also shows that there is a smaller proportion of older men living alone (below 10% within each age group). From just above 4% in the 65–69 age group, the proportion increases as they get older before reaching the peak at around 6.8–9.3% when they reach above the age of 80. An exception to this is Cambodia where only 0.9% of men in their 80s live alone.

In Myanmar, depending on the age group, around 14.3–28.2% of older persons aged 60+ live alone (Teerawichitchainan et al., 2015, p. 1341) while in Singapore, about 8% of older persons aged 65+ live alone (Department of Statistics, 2011).

The percentage of the older adults living alone in Southeast Asia is still lower compared with the rest of Asia, although the numbers are close to China where about 9% (Lei et al., 2015, p. 195) to 12% (Ren & Treiman, 2015, p. 265) of people aged 60+ are living alone. Southeast Asian figures are also lower than the 2010 figures for Korea where the number of older adults living alone has radically risen in the past decades. From just 5% in 1980, the percentage of women aged 65+ who live alone in 2010 has reached 30%, or a 500% increase in 30 years, while men registered a 400% increase within the same period of time (Park & Choi, 2015, pp. 1187–1188).

References

Asis, M. M., Domingo, L., Knodel, J., & Mehta, K. (1995). Living arrangements in four Asian countries: A comparative perspective. *Journal of Cross-Cultural Gerontology, 10*(1–2), 145–162.

Department of Statistics. (2011). *Singapore census of population 2010*. Retrieved from http://www.singstat.gov.sg/publications/publications-and-papers/cop2010/census10_stat_release1

Dommaraju, P., & Tan, J. (2014). Households in contemporary Southeast Asia. *Journal of Comparative Family Studies, 45*(4), 559–580.

Esteve, A., & Liu, C. (2014). *Families in Asia: A cross-national comparison of intergenerational co-residence*. Paper presented at the International Cyberseminar: Family demography: Advancing knowledge about intergenerational relationships and exchanges in low and middle-income countries, Cyberseminar. http://blog.soton.ac.uk/intergen/files/2014/01/Esteve_Liu_Families-in-Asia_IUSSP_Cyberseminar.pdf

Knodel, J., & Nguyen, M. D. (2015). Grandparents and grandchildren: Care and support in Myanmar, Thailand and Vietnam. *Ageing and Society, 35*(09), 1960–1988. https://doi.org/10.1017/S0144686X14000786

Lei, X., Strauss, J., Tian, M., & Zhao, Y. (2015). Living arrangements of the elderly in China: Evidence from the CHARLS national baseline. *China Economic Journal, 8*(3), 191. https://doi.org/10.1080/17538963.2015.1102473

Mehta, K., Osman, M. M., & Alexander, L. E. Y. (1995). Living arrangements of the elderly in Singapore: Cultural norms in transition. *Journal of Cross-Cultural Gerontology, 10*(1), 113–143. https://doi.org/10.1007/bf00972033

Ministry of Social and Family Development. (2015). *Ageing families in Singapore*. Retrieved from https://www.msf.gov.sg/research-and-data/Research-and-Data-Series/Documents/Ageing%20Families%20Report%20Insight%20Series%2020151124.pdf

Park, H., & Choi, J. (2015). Long-term trends in living alone among Korean adults: Age, gender, and educational differences. *Demographic Research, 32*, 1177–1208. https://doi.org/10.4054/DemRes.2015.32.43

Podhisita, C., & Xenos, P. (2015). Living alone in South and Southeast Asia: An analysis of census data. *Demographic Research, 32*, 41. https://doi.org/10.4054/DemRes.2015.32.41

Ren, Q., & Treiman, D. J. (2015). Living arrangements of the elderly in China and consequences for their emotional well-being. *Chinese Sociological Review, 47*(3), 255. https://doi.org/10.1080/21620555.2015.1032162

Teerawichitchainan, B., Knodel, J., & Pothisiri, W. (2015). What does living alone really mean for older persons? A comparative study of Myanmar, Vietnam, and Thailand. *Demographic Research, 32*, 48. https://doi.org/10.4054/DemRes.2015.32.48

Voon Chin, P., & Loh, J. (2008). Filial piety and intergenerational co-residence: The case of Chinese Singaporeans. *Asian Journal of Social Science, 36*(3/4), 659–679.

Wong, Y. S., & Verbrugge, L. M. (2009). Living alone: Elderly Chinese Singaporeans. *Journal of Cross-Cultural Gerontology, 24*(3), 209–224. https://doi.org/10.1007/s10823-008-9081-7

Yeung, W.-J. J., & Cheung, A. K.-L. (2015). Living alone: One-person households in Asia. *Demographic Research, 32*, 40.https://doi.org/10.4054/DemRes.2015.32.40

Open Access This chapter is licensed under the terms of the Creative Commons Attribution 4.0 International License (http://creativecommons.org/licenses/by/4.0/), which permits use, sharing, adaptation, distribution and reproduction in any medium or format, as long as you give appropriate credit to the original author(s) and the source, provide a link to the Creative Commons license and indicate if changes were made.

The images or other third party material in this chapter are included in the chapter's Creative Commons license, unless indicated otherwise in a credit line to the material. If material is not included in the chapter's Creative Commons license and your intended use is not permitted by statutory regulation or exceeds the permitted use, you will need to obtain permission directly from the copyright holder.

Part II
Child and Youth Well-Being

Part II shows changes over time in indicators of education, employment, and health that are pertinent to children and youth's well-being.

Part II
Trade and Young ICT Firms

Chapter 6
Education and Youth Unemployment in Southeast Asia

6.1 Youth Literacy Rates

The Universal Declaration of Human Rights sees education or literacy as a human right. The World Declaration on Education for All, endorsed by UNESCO, is committed to achieving education for all citizens in every society, while the Dakar Framework for Action is helping to achieve this aim. Literacy gives rise to more opportunities in life and is the key to development and empowerment.

From Fig. 6.1, youth literacy rates among countries are generally on the rise. Southeast Asian countries (except Laos and Cambodia) are doing well in youth (15–24 years old) literacy, with rates above 95% since 1990, significantly higher than the world's average of 89.5% (UIS, 2013). This means that a large majority of youths in Southeast Asia "are able to read and write with understanding a short simple statement about their everyday life" (UNESCO).[1] Thailand and Indonesia, however, are showing worrying signs of a downward trend since around 2005.

Singapore and Brunei top the other countries with a literacy rate of 99.8% in 2012. Singapore's success in attaining a high literacy rate is a pragmatic strategy. The lack of natural resources compelled Singapore to rely on investing and raising its human capital (Lee et al., 2008).

Considerable progress can be seen in Cambodia and Laos with raising literacy rates among youths. Both countries managed to raise their literacy rates by 10 percentage points from the mid-1990s to the mid-2000s. This reflects increasing access to education among the younger generations. Nonetheless, Cambodia and Laos still fall short of the world's average, with literacy rates at 87.1% in 2009 and 83.9% in 2005, respectively. A slowdown in the improvement of literacy rates in Cambodia from 2009 is observed. Part of the reason lies in the limited reach of ethnic minorities and the population that resides in the rural areas. The challenge now is thus to raise the youth literary rates to a sustainable state by reducing gender disparities in education and increasing access to education in rural areas.

---

[1] Source: http://uis.unesco.org/en/glossary-term/youth-literacy-rate accessed on 18 July 2017.

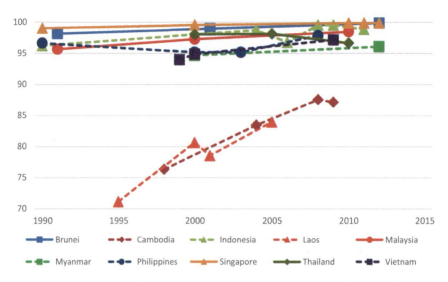

Fig. 6.1 Literacy rates of 15–24-year-olds in Southeast Asia, 1990–2012. *Source* Millennium Development Goals, accessed on 28 November 2016. *Notes* Latest available data for Indonesia refer to 2011, for Malaysia and Thailand to 2010, for Cambodia and Vietnam to 2009, for the Philippines to 2008, and for Laos to 2005. No available data for Timor-Leste

6.2 Expected Years in Full-Time Education

The expected years in full-time education are defined as the number of years of schooling that a child of school entrance age can expect to receive if prevailing patterns of age-specific enrolment rates persist throughout the child's life. Figure 6.2 shows a steady increase in expected years in full-time education for all Southeast Asian countries. Singapore takes the lead with an expected time of 15.4 years in full-time education in 2013, Brunei has a similar trend, while Myanmar lags with only an expected of 8.6 years in full-time education.

An analysis done on OECD indicators (OECD, 2014a) showed that it is expected that a person spends 9.4 years in primary and lower secondary education, 3.4 years for upper secondary, and the rest on post-secondary non-tertiary education and tertiary education. Based on this analysis, a child born in Brunei, Indonesia, Malaysia, Singapore, or Thailand can be expected to receive full-time education up till the upper secondary level. As for Cambodia, Laos, Philippines, Timor-Leste, and Vietnam, their expected years in full-time education range from 10 to 12 years.

However, the expected years in full-time education for Myanmar are worrying. Myanmar had an expected year in full-time education of 6 years in 1980 and grew by around two years to reach an expected year of full-time education of 8.3 years in 2005, but since then there has only been a very small increase—to 8.6 years in 2013. It is the only country in Southeast Asia that has an expected year of below 10 years, and this means that a child is not expected to complete his lower secondary education. The lack of education could impede Myanmar's economic growth. With

6.2 Expected Years in Full-Time Education

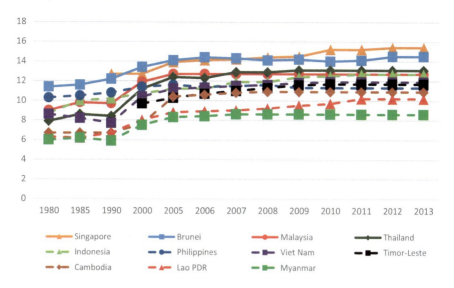

Fig. 6.2 Expected years in full-time education in Southeast Asia, 1980–2013. *Source* UNESCO Institute for Statistics, accessed on 21 June 2017

the changing economic conditions and the world moving towards technology-based industries, a minimum qualification in upper secondary education is essential in preparing an individual for the working world (OECD, 2004).

As for the Philippines, although it started as a country that has the highest education level in Southeast Asia—with an expected of 10.3 years in full-time education in 1980, it did not manage to improve much over the years. The Philippines had the smallest increase in expected years of only one year (11.3 years in 2013), and several other countries overtook it as the years passed such as Thailand, Malaysia, Indonesia, Vietnam, and Timor-Leste.

On the other hand, Thailand was quite the opposite of the Philippines. It saw a spike from 7.9 years in 1980 to 13.1 years in 2013 and is one of the countries with the highest expected years in full-time education, just behind Singapore and Brunei. This could be due to the changes in the sectoral composition of the economy which led to an increase in the returns of education for Thailand. Its high growth rate and the emphasis on the service sector raised the demand for skilled labour and thus the demand for higher education. This shift, together with the National Education Act in 1999 that provides free twelve years of education to its people, explained the rapid rise in expected years of education for Thailand (Blunch, 2016).

6.3 Rate of Out-Of-School Children of Primary School Age

UNESCO defines the rate of out-of-school children (OOSC) of primary school age as the number of children of official primary school age who are not enrolled in primary or secondary school, expressed as a percentage of the population of official primary school age.

Figure 6.3 shows a general downward trend for the rate of OOSC of primary school age in all Southeast Asian countries. Brunei, Vietnam, and the Philippines were doing pretty well in the 1970s with rates of below 10%, while Myanmar and Indonesia had rates that are at the higher end (38% and 30%, respectively). By 2011, all countries with available data had rates of OOSC below 10%. Myanmar, Indonesia, and Malaysia show a particularly impressive decline. However, despite the low rates, Thailand, Malaysia, Indonesia, Cambodia, Timor-Leste, and Vietnam are showing signs of an increasing trend from the 2010s.

Vietnam and the Philippines are the two countries with a substantially low rate of OOSC in the mid-1970s of below 5%. However, the rate in the Philippines fluctuated a fair bit throughout the years and even increased a little since 1977. UNESCO reported in its National Education Support Strategy that the quality of elementary education in the Philippines has been declining over the years and there is an underinvestment in educational resources (UNESCO, 2009). These resulted in low scores that had an impact on the increase in dropout rates. However, the implementation

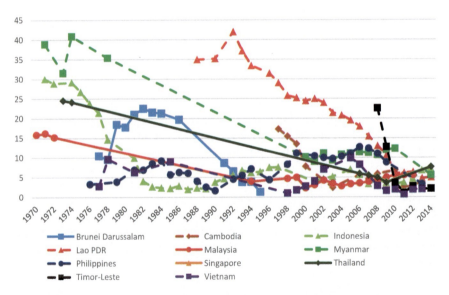

Fig. 6.3 Rate of out-of-school children of primary school age, 1970–2014. *Source* UNESCO Institute for Statistics, accessed on 28 November 2016. *Notes* Latest available data for Vietnam and the Philippines refer to 2013, for Malaysia to 2012, and for Brunei Darussalam to 1995. No available data for Singapore

of a conditional cash transfer (CCT) policy required families on the receiving end to send their children to school (David & Albert, 2015). The effectiveness of such an implementation is reflected in a steady decline in OOSC rate, where it decreased from 12.3% in 2007 to 3.25% in 2013.

Timor-Leste had one of the steepest drops for OOSC rate. It saw a dip from 22.6% in 2008 to 2.2% in 2014. This may suggest that the government's aim to provide free basic education for all children since 2005 had been an effective strategy to bring children back to school (Saikia et al., 2011).

An unusual pattern is observed for Brunei. Its rate of OOSC is concaved downwards for the years with available data (1977–1995). The maximum rate was in 1983 at 21.4% and started declining thereafter.

When the data are stratified into gender (data not shown), the trends for the rate of OOSC of primary school age are similar to the overall data in Fig. 6.3. A notable difference is that the rate of OOSC of primary school age for females is generally higher than males except for Brunei. Brunei shows the reverse where females have a slightly lower rate compared to males.

In Timor-Leste, the rate of OOSC for females went down in the 2010s but went up instead for males. A study by Justino et al. (2013) revealed that violence in Timor-Leste undermines educational achievements for males, but not females, in the long run. This was attributed to cultural norms around perceived gender roles. Boys are expected to work and fill in the gaps of dead or disabled male adults involved in the violence, restricting them from going to school. Timor-Leste experienced a conflict in 2006 that could have caused the phenomenon of an increasing rate of out-of-school males in the 2010s.

6.4 Transition Rate from Primary to Lower Secondary Education

The effective transition rate from primary to lower secondary education is the number of new entrants to the first grade of lower secondary education in the following year expressed as a percentage of the students enrolled in the last grade of primary education in the given year who do not repeat that grade the following year. From Fig. 6.4, it can be seen that the rates have risen considerably in Southeast Asia. However, there was a decline in Malaysia since 2000 and some small fluctuations in Indonesia and Cambodia in recent years.

The downward trend for Malaysia came as a surprise as the Malaysian government made strides in democratizing lower secondary education in 1964. The government got rid of the secondary school entrance examination, which allowed all primary school students to progress to lower secondary education. This move could be the reason for the highly effective transition rate of 99.2% for Malaysia in 2000 (Fig. 6.4). Unfortunately, few studies have gone into the phenomenon of this falling effective

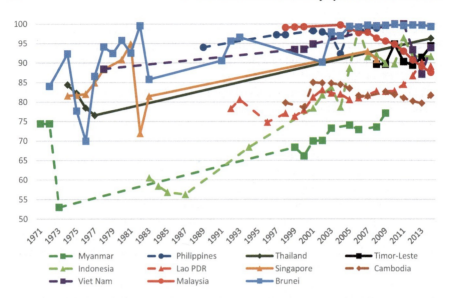

Fig. 6.4 Effective transition rate from primary to lower secondary general education in Southeast Asia, 1971–2014. *Source* UNESCO Institute for Statistics, accessed on 20 June 2017

transition rate in Malaysia. Nonetheless, it may be that parents are enrolling their children into alternative institutions, such as faith-based schools, for secondary education (Malaysia EFA Status Report, 2011). Data for these institutions are difficult to collect, and thus, the government is unable to have complete information on students transiting to alternative schools after primary education.

Malaysia is not the only country seeing a decrease in effective transition rate from primary to lower secondary education. Cambodia, Timor-Leste, and Vietnam are also displaying signs of a downward trend from the 2000s onwards. This is perplexing as actions had been taken by international organizations and the local governments to provide education for children. The decreasing trend could mean that efforts by the organizations and government had ceased or their effects have diminished.

Nonetheless, Myanmar and Indonesia had a huge leap in their effective transition rate from 1975 to 2010. Indonesia managed to go from 60.5% in 1980 to 91.7% in 2014, nearly on par with the other high-achieving Southeast Asia countries. As for Myanmar, although it is still far behind the other countries with a rate of less than 80%, it saw a 24% jump from 1975 (53%) to 2010 (77%). Myanmar provides only free primary school education, which could be the reason for the relatively low effective transition rate to lower secondary. The government had been increasing efforts to battle this dismal rate by increasing stipends to households, thereby encouraging students to stay in school and move on to the secondary school level. Another reason is due to lack of proximity for secondary schools, especially in the rural areas (OECD, 2014b). The recent expansion of secondary schools and the implementation of free education for lower secondary in 2014 could mean that Myanmar will be seeing progress in its effective transition rate.

6.5 Gross Secondary Enrolment Ratio

Southeast Asian countries saw a huge leap in gross secondary school enrolment ratio from 1970 to 2015. From Fig. 6.5, most countries with available data in the 1970s had an average of 20% gross secondary enrolment rate and achieved a rate of above 50% by 2015 (except for Cambodia with a rate of 45% in 2008). Singapore and Thailand went over a rate of a hundred per cent, which is a statistical artefact indicating cases of either early or late school entrance and grade repetition.

The steepest jump in the ratio is Thailand, which went from 18.1% in 1971 to 129% in 2015. This increase is due mainly to the efforts of the government body in the 1980s, which saw the need to increase secondary education. The Thai government targeted schooling affordability by waiving school fees and providing uniforms and textbooks. It also improved accessibility to secondary schools by establishing secondary classes in existing primary schools in rural areas (John, 1997).

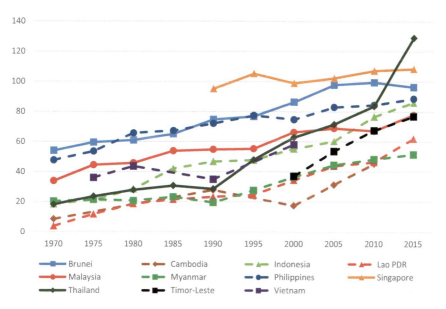

Fig. 6.5 Gross secondary enrolment ratio in Southeast Asia for both sexes, 1970–2015. *Source* UNESCO Institute for Statistics, accessed on 24 July 2017, except for Singapore. Data for Singapore retrieved from http://data.gov.sg on 24 July 2017. *Notes* For Brunei, data for 1990 are actually from 1991 and for 1995 from 1994; for Thailand, data for 1970 from 1971 and for 2000 from 2001; for Indonesia, data for 1980 from 1981 and for 1985 from 1986; for the Philippines, data for 1970 from 1971, for 2000 from 2001, for 2010 from 2009, and for 2015 from 2013; for Vietnam, data for 1975 from 1976 and for 2000 from 1998; for Timor-Leste, data for 2000 from 2001; for Cambodia, data for 1970 from 1971, for 1990 from 1991, for 2005 from 2004, and for 2010 from 2008; for Lao, data for 1970 from 1971 and for 1975 from 1977; for Myanmar, data for 1970 from 1971, for 1975 from 1976, and for 2015 from 2014. Latest available data for Cambodia refer to 2010 and for Vietnam refer to 2000

Myanmar on the other hand is moving at a slower pace compared to other countries such as Indonesia and Thailand that started with around the same enrolment rate as it. It grew from 20% in 1971 to only 51% in 2014, whereas Indonesia and Thailand hit a rate of 86% and 129%, respectively, in 2015. Even Laos, which started at a miserable secondary school enrolment ratio of 3.7% in 1971, overtook Myanmar in the 2010s with a rate of 61.7% in 2015. The relatively low secondary school enrolment rate is attributed to the weak education system in Myanmar and that the curriculum does not cater to children who are and will be going into the agricultural sector (Skidmore & Wilson, 2008). This led to a high dropout rate starting from primary school, which eventually affected the enrolment ratio for secondary school.

A notable trend is Cambodia, which saw its secondary enrolment ratio climbing steadily up through the 1970s and 1980s. However, after 1991, there was a dip from 27.8% to 16.5% in the 1990s before Cambodia went back on track and started to rise again (to 45.1 in 2010).

6.6 Gender Parity Index (GPI) in Southeast Asia

Millennium Development Goals compute gender parity index (GPI) for primary, secondary, and tertiary enrolment by dividing female gross enrolment ratio by male gross enrolment ratio for each relevant category. A GPI of 1.0 (or within 0.97 and 1.03) indicates parity between girls and boys. A GPI above 1.0 indicates a disparity to the disadvantage of boys, while a GPI below 1.0 indicates a disparity to the disadvantage of girls.

6.6.1 GPI for Primary School Enrolment

Female and male gross enrolment rates are converging among Southeast Asian countries. Figure 6.6 shows that although there are slight fluctuations throughout the years, gender parity in primary enrolment has been largely achieved in this area. Indonesia, Vietnam, Thailand, Singapore, and the Philippines have observed a GPI close to 1.0 since the 1990s. Myanmar and Brunei managed to improve their GPI to between 0.97 and 0.99 and achieved stable gender parity by 2000.

On the other hand, Malaysia had been doing well between 1990 and 2002 in maintaining gender parity but saw a decline since 2003. The last available data in 2005 (0.94) showed that Malaysia had dipped below the recommended parity index of 0.97.

Gender inequality for primary enrolment is still evident in Laos and Cambodia. Their GPI in the 1990s was below 0.85, much lower compared to other countries. However, we see substantial improvements in both countries in terms of narrowing the gender gap, from roughly 0.8–0.95 within the 24 years. A steady increase in GPI to reach gender parity since 1990 in these two countries could be attributed to international pressure to address the gender inequality in primary education. In Cambodia,

6.6 Gender Parity Index (GPI) in Southeast Asia

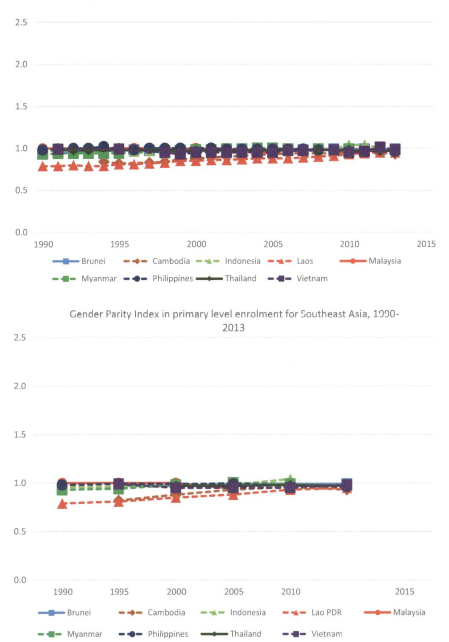

Fig. 6.6 Gender parity index for primary-level enrolment of Southeast Asia, 1990–2013. *Source* Millennium Development Goals, accessed on 28 November 2016. *Notes* Latest available data for Indonesia refer to 2012, for Myanmar to 2010, and for Malaysia to 2005. Data are not available for Singapore and Timor-Leste

on top of government efforts, international organizations such as UNICEF rendered aid by providing funds to reduce the costs of education, encouraging education in both boys and girls (Booth, 2016). For Laos, government intervention with the aim of equitable access to primary education resulted in the increase in primary school enrolment, from 58% in 1991 to 89% in 2008. This phenomenon is mainly due to the rise in female enrolment, which significantly closed the gap in gender inequality for primary enrolment (Onphanhdala & Suruga, 2010).

Despite these advances in GPI, Laos and Cambodia still fall short of achieving gender parity, which could be due to cultural norms. For example, research shows that in Cambodia, due to deeply entrenched gender roles, women are expected to remain behind men in terms of education (Booth, 2016). This results in a lack of educational opportunities for women, and increasing gender disparity is observed in higher levels of education.

6.6.2 GPI for Secondary School Enrolment

From Fig. 6.7, we see that GPI for secondary enrolment varies widely in the region, with disparities to the disadvantage of boys in some countries and the disadvantage of girls in others.

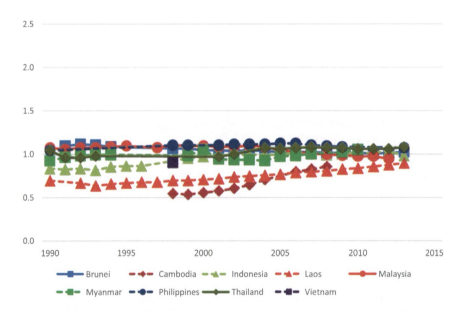

Fig. 6.7 Gender parity index for secondary-level enrolment of Southeast Asia, 1990–2013. *Source* Millennium Development Goals, accessed on 28 November 2016. *Notes* Latest available data for Malaysia refer to 2012, for Myanmar to 2010, for Cambodia to 2009, and for Vietnam to 2008. Data not available for Singapore and Timor-Leste

Similar to GPI in primary enrolment, Laos and Cambodia have made a tremendous stride in closing the gender gaps in secondary enrolment. However, as mentioned, the gender gap still exists and is greater than in primary enrolment (Fig. 6.7). Laos had a GPI of 0.89 in 2013, and Cambodia had a GPI of 0.85 in 2008, with signs of decrease.

Looking at the same figure, gender gaps have reversed in secondary enrolment for the Philippines, Myanmar, Malaysia, and Thailand. The latest data in 2013 show boys are at a disadvantage in terms of secondary-level enrolment with GPIs of 1.07, 1.05, and 1.08, respectively. This situation suggests the possibility of different existing gender roles having an impact on the differential education level between boys and girls. For example, boys from low-income families in the Philippines drop out during the transition to secondary school to contribute to household income (UNICEF, 2009).

Malaysia started with a GPI of 1.07 in 1990. Over the years, it managed to decrease its GPI and attain gender parity in 2006. However, the drop in GPI continued and the initial disadvantage to boys shifted to a disadvantage to girls at secondary-level enrolment.

Singapore, Indonesia, and Brunei are the only Southeast Asian countries that have achieved gender parity in secondary enrolment. However, it is important to bear in mind that these values reflect trends at the national level. GPI at regional levels, especially for larger countries like Indonesia, might reflect a different reality where gender disparity continues to exist in specific segments of rural and urban areas.

6.6.3 GPI for Tertiary School Enrolment

Figure 6.8 shows that the GPI for tertiary school enrolment among Southeast Asian countries depicts a polarizing trend: half the countries had GPI above 1, signifying gender disparity to the disadvantage of boys, while the other half had GPI below 1, signifying the reverse. Despite the case, almost all countries seem to be converging towards gender parity.

Brunei, with an average GPI of 1.74, is the exception with females enrolled outnumbering males by a considerable margin (between 15 and 20% over the years since 1995). This significant difference in tertiary enrolment between the two genders can be explained by girls outdoing boys in mathematics and English during pre-tertiary education, where a good performance in both subjects is essential in getting a tertiary education (Metussin, 2017).

Malaysia, the Philippines, Myanmar, and Thailand see a consistent GPI of above 1.2. In Malaysia, the government prioritized education when it saw the economic success neighbouring countries had achieved with high education. This sustained investment in education led to a narrowing of the gender gap and even resulted in male education lagging behind that of females (Asadullah, 2014). Although not much research has been done regarding this phenomenon in this region, OECD (2008)

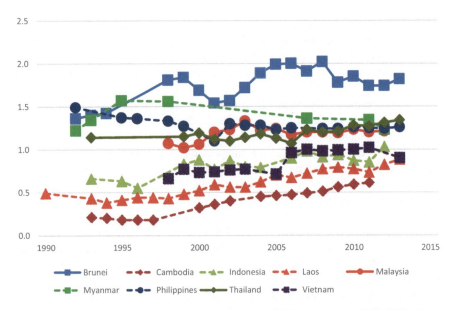

Fig. 6.8 Gender parity index for tertiary-level enrolment of Southeast Asia, 1990–2013. *Source* Millennium Development Goals, accessed on 28 November 2016. *Notes* Latest available data for Indonesia, Malaysia, and Myanmar refer to 2012, for Myanmar to 2010, and for Cambodia to 2011. Data not available for Singapore and Timor-Leste

suggests that the reversal in gender inequality can be attributed to the higher pay-off that females obtain compared to males between a graduate and non-graduate.

As for Singapore, it managed to raise its GPI from 0.77 in 1990 to achieving gender parity in 2005. Since then, its GPI had risen steadily, reached an all-time high of 1.1 in 2011, and then dropped to 1.08 in 2013, closing the disparity gap.

6.7 Gender Differences in University Graduates by Fields of Study

Females have been enrolled in all different kinds of field in tertiary education. The enrolment in agriculture, forestry, fisheries, and veterinary has decreased most notably in Malaysia (Fig. 6.9). Enrolment in education, arts, and social sciences remains high. In Brunei, the female enrolment rates in information technology, health and welfare, and natural sciences are high, whereas enrolment in engineering, manufacturing, and construction remains significantly lower. Females in the Philippines and Malaysia also have high rates of health and welfare. There is a notable increase for Malaysian females to specialize in natural sciences, mathematics, and statistics since 2005.

6.7 Gender Differences in University Graduates by Fields of Study

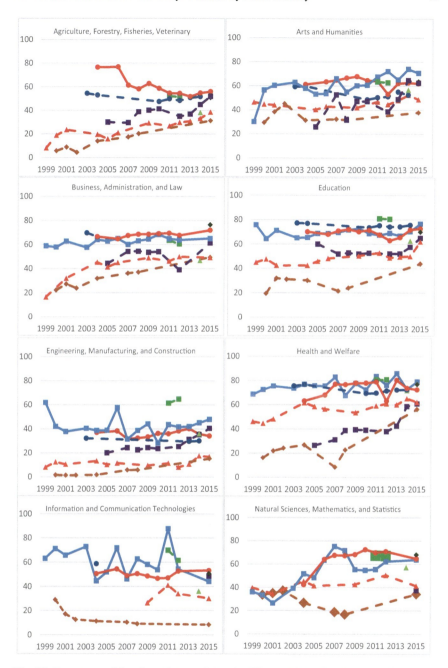

Fig. 6.9 Percentage of female tertiary graduates in different fields of study in Southeast Asia, 1999–2015. *Source* UNESCO Institute for Statistics, accessed on 21 June 2017. *Note* No data for Singapore and Timor-Leste

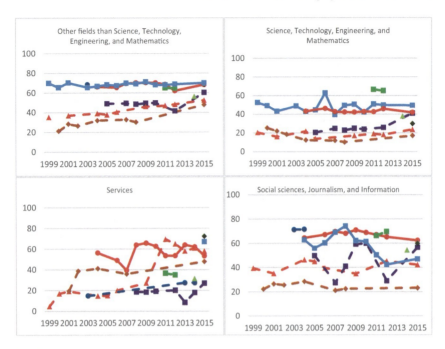

Fig. 6.9 (continued)

6.8 Population with at least Completed Upper Secondary Education

There is a general increasing trend in the proportion of the population aged 25 and above with at least completed upper secondary education in Southeast Asian countries. The percentage attainment varies widely among countries, with Singapore having the highest percentage of 69.5% in 2014 and Cambodia having the lowest with 6.3% in 2009 (Fig. 6.10). A survey done by OECD concluded that upper secondary education plays an important role in preparing young people with the minimum level of education to become productive members of the workforce (OECD, 2004).

The level of educational attainment can be linked to the level of development in the country. Developed countries place much emphasis on higher education levels. Singapore, irrefutably the most developed country in Southeast Asia, is a good example in this case. Singapore has developed rapidly since its independence in 1965, shifting from a labour-intensive economy to a knowledge-based economy. The economic transformation thereby required a highly trained workforce. This resulted in a large and rising percentage of the population receiving at least upper secondary education to gain the necessary knowledge and skills required to drive the economy (Murray et al., 1980).

For developing countries, education reforms can be said to be the main driver of the rising percentage of the population to have obtained at least upper secondary

6.8 Population with at least Completed Upper Secondary Education

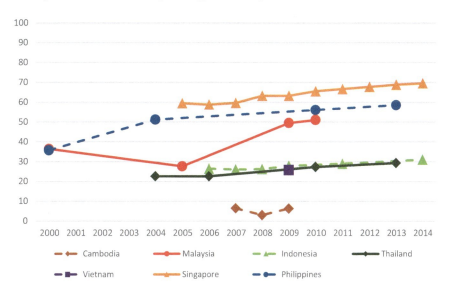

Fig. 6.10 Percentage of population age 25+ with at least completed upper secondary education in Southeast Asia, 2000–2014. *Source* World Bank, accessed on 21 June 2017. *Notes* Latest available data for Indonesia and Thailand refer to 2013, for Malaysia to 2010, and for Vietnam and Cambodia to 2009. Data not available for Brunei, Lao PDR, Myanmar, and Timor-Leste

education. The 1988 free public secondary education act in the Philippines and four other reforms thereafter allowed for the increase. The segregation of cohorts before and after the implementation of the policy saw the latter cohort benefitting from the policy with a much higher percentage of people having completed upper secondary compared to the former (Revilla & Laarni, 2014).

On the other hand, the changes in the sectoral composition of the economy led to an increase in the returns of education for Thailand. Its high growth rate and the emphasis on the service sector raised the demand for skilled labour and thus the demand for higher education. This shift, together with the National Education Act in 1999 that provides free twelve years of education to its people, explained the increasing percentage of the population that had completed upper secondary education (Blunch, 2016). Indonesia followed a similar trend. Nevertheless, the percentages in both countries remain low at around 30% in 2013.

Malaysia saw a decline in the percentage of the population having at least completed upper secondary education from 35.7% in 2000 to 27.6% in 2005 but managed to climb back up after 2005 to reach a comparable percentage to the Philippines in 2009.

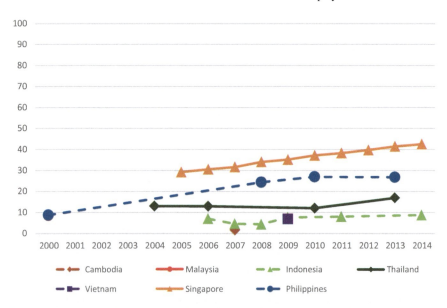

Fig. 6.11 Percentage of population age 25+ with at least completed tertiary education in Southeast Asia, 2000–2014. *Source* World Bank, accessed on 21 June 2017. *Notes* Latest available data for the Philippines and Thailand refer to 2013, for Vietnam to 2009, for Cambodia to 2007, and for Malaysia to 2000. Data not available for Brunei, Lao PDR, Myanmar, and Timor-Leste

6.9 Population with at least Completed Tertiary Education

The trend for the percentage of population aged 25 and above with at least completed tertiary education (Fig. 6.11) is similar to that of completed upper secondary education (Fig. 6.10). Countries that reflect a high percentage for upper secondary education correspond with a high percentage for tertiary education and vice versa. However, the proportion of population that had at least completed tertiary education is lower than for upper secondary education. As economies continue to develop, there will be an increase in demand for higher educated workers.

In Singapore, there is a limited proportion of graduates from each cohort that is capped at 30–40%. This is to prevent the oversaturation of graduates and ensures that the education system is in line with the needs of the economy. Figure 6.11 shows the trend of an increase in the population who completed tertiary education from 29.1% in 2005 to 42.4% in 2014 with signs of a slowing increase. Singapore is looking to increasing university places by another 3000 in 2020 to accommodate the increasing demand for university education.[2]

As for the other Southeast Asian countries, the proportion of the population with a completed tertiary education is below 30%. This is not surprising given that they are still developing and their economies are largely driven by labour-intensive sectors

---

[2] Straits Times (18 May 2013).

such as agriculture and manufacturing. However, countries like Thailand and the Philippines have started shifting away from these labour-intensive sectors to high-skill services, thereby increasing the demand for university graduates (Mehta et al., 2013). Therefore, there is a need to align the education system and prepare the population for the change. This is reflected by the gradual increase in the per cent of the population aged 25 and above with at least completed tertiary education.

The Philippines saw a gradual rise in the per cent of the population with completed tertiary education from 8.6% in 2000 to 26.8% in 2010 and has thereafter remained stagnant. There is a slight drop in percentage in Thailand from 2004 (13%) to 2010 (12%), before starting to rise steadily till 16.9% in 2013. The increase in the per cent of the population obtaining tertiary education is due to the Thai government prioritizing investment in education, budgeting an average of 4% of their GDP since 2000, and expanding tertiary education opportunities (Paweenawat & Vechbanyongratana, 2015). This percentage remains lower than 10% in Indonesia and Vietnam. Data on Cambodia, only available in 2007, show that only 1.5% of the 25 and older had completed the tertiary education at that time.

6.10 Youth Unemployment in Southeast Asia

Youth unemployment refers to the share of the labour force aged 15–24 without work but available for and seeking employment. According to International Labour Organization (2015), global youth unemployment rates have been fluctuating between 11.7 and 13.2% from 1995 to 2015. As shown in Fig. 6.12b, c, youth unemployment rates vary across the different countries in the region, but female youth unemployment rates are generally higher than that of males. As a region, Southeast Asia has a high youth unemployment rate which is mostly driven by the high rate in Indonesia, the Philippines, and Timor-Leste.

Throughout the past decades, Indonesia, the Philippines, and Timor-Leste have had youth unemployment rates that were higher than the global rates (Fig. 6.12a). The Philippines and Timor-Leste recorded similar patterns of fluctuations, but youth unemployment rates were generally higher in the Philippines. Youth unemployment rates in the Philippines fluctuated between 15 and 24.8% from 1990 to 2015, while youth unemployment rates in Timor-Leste fluctuated between 12 and 16.5% within the same period (Fig. 6.12a).

High youth unemployment rates in Timor-Leste could be attributed to political and civil disturbances that began before its independence in 2002 (Saldanha & Redden, 2009). The unrest led to the collapse of civil service, the displacement of individuals including professionals and the contraction of its economy (Saldanha & Redden, 2009). As a young nation, job prospects for young people in Timor-Leste remain largely limited (Saldanha & Redden, 2009).

As for the Philippines, its consistently weak per-capita GDP growth (Fig. 2.8a) suggests limited employment opportunities for its young population. Despite the latter, the Philippines observed declining youth unemployment rates from 2000 to

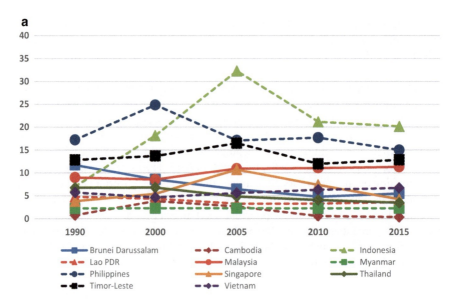

Fig. 6.12a Youth (aged 15–24) unemployment rates in Southeast Asia, 1990–2015 (% of total labour force)

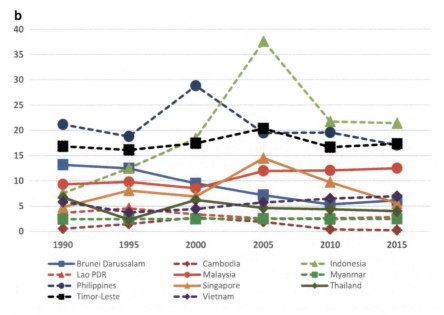

Fig. 6.12b Female youth (aged 15–24) unemployment rates in Southeast Asia, 1990–2015 (% of total labour force)

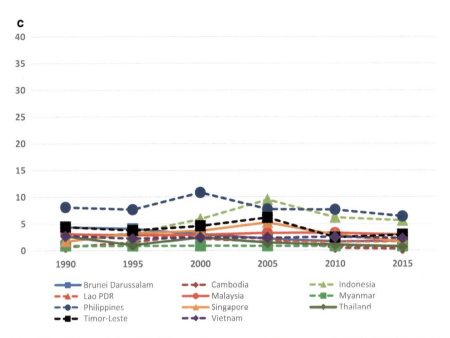

Fig. 6.12c Male youth (aged 15–24) unemployment rates in Southeast Asia, 1990–2015 (% of total labour force). *Source* International Labour Organization, ILOSTAT database, accessed on March 2017

2015, which could be attributed to the growth in the country's service sector (Bank, 2011). Furthermore, female youth employment rates were also disproportionately higher than that of male youth unemployment rates in the Philippines (Fig. 6.12b, c). With reference to Fig. 2.12, the limited participation of women in the Philippines' labour market may be attributed to its relatively high GII values ranging from 0.4 to 0.5.

Indonesia was badly hurt by the Asian financial crisis in 1997. Its youth unemployment rate observed an accelerated growth of 14.1% from 2000 to 2005, before surpassing the Philippines and Timor-Leste with the highest youth unemployment rate of 32.3% in 2005. According to Comola and De Mello (2011), Indonesia went through a process of fiscal decentralization in 2001, which resulted in a sharp increase in its minimum wage. Employers were therefore deterred from employing youths, for most were usually without job experiences (Comola & De Mello, 2011; Pratomo, 2016). Within the same period, female youth unemployment in Indonesia observed a greater increase as compared to male unemployment; Indonesia's female youth unemployment rate increased by 19.2% (Fig. 6.12b), while the male youth unemployment rate increased only by 3.6% (Fig. 6.12c). The dominating perception of women as the secondary earners in Indonesia may have driven female unemployment, especially during the 2001 fiscal decentralization (Oey-Gardiner & Sulastri, 2000 as cited in Utomo, 2012). Despite a decline of 12.1% from 2005 to 2015,

Indonesia remained the country with the highest youth unemployment rate in the region (Fig. 6.12a).

The other Southeast Asian countries have had youth unemployment rates lower than that of global rates (Fig. 6.12a). It is interesting to note that Singapore and Brunei, the only developed countries in Southeast Asia, have observed higher youth unemployment rates as compared to Thailand, Lao PDR, Myanmar, and Cambodia from 1990 to 2015.

Singapore recorded a climb of 5.30% in youth unemployment rates from 2000 to 2005, possibly due to the 1998 Asian Financial Crisis, before a steady decline from 10.70% in 2005 to 4.20% in 2015, as the economy recovered and grew (Fig. 6.12a). Brunei, on the other hand, began to experience a steady decline from 11.72% in 1990 to 4.77% in 2010 (Fig. 6.12a). According to Roberts (2011), there was a conscious effort made by the current Sultan to generate employment by expanding the agricultural and government sector. Brunei also observed a notable decline of 7.87% in the female youth unemployment rate from 1990 to 2010 (Fig. 6.12b), possibly due to increased governmental efforts to ensure equal educational opportunities for women; for instance, 65.0% of 2838 students studying at the University of Brunei Darussalam in 2010 were females (Government of Brunei Darussalam, 2001 as cited in Anaman & Kassim, 2006).

Lao PDR, Myanmar, and Cambodia have had the lowest youth unemployment rates in the region (Fig. 6.12a). By 2015, Cambodia had the lowest youth unemployment rate of 0.30% in the region (Fig. 6.12a). The latter could be attributed to Cambodia's growing agriculture and service sectors that have been significant sources of youth employment (Elder, 2014 as cited in McKay et al., 2018).

It is crucial to note that the data sets do not take into account the large numbers of Southeast Asian youths working in informal sectors, i.e. subsistence agriculture, and temporary or casual jobs (McKay et al., 2018; Saldanha & Redden, 2009).

References

Anaman, K. A., & Kassim, H. M. (2006). Marriage and female labour supply in Brunei Darussalam: A case study of urban women in Bandar Seri Begawan. *The Journal of Socio-Economics, 35*(5), 797–812. https://doi.org/10.1016/j.socec.2005.11.038

Asadullah, M. N. (2014). Gender gap in education is result of policy priorities. *The Korea Herald.* Retrieved from https://umexpert.um.edu.my/file/publication/00013115_111962.pdf

Bank, W. (2011). *2011 Philippines development report: Generating inclusive growth to uplift the poor.* World Bank U6 - ctx_ver=Z39.88-2004&ctx_enc=info%3Aofi%2Fenc%3AUTF-8&rfr_id=info%3Asid%2Fsummon.serialssolutions.com&rft_val_fmt=info%3Aofi%2Ffmt%3Akev%3Amtx%3Abook&rft.genre=book&rft.title=2011+Philippines+Development+Report + %3A+Generating+Inclusive+Growth+to+Uplift+the+Poor&rft.au=World+Bank&rft.date=2011-02-01&rft.pub=World+Bank&rft.externalDBID=n%2Fa&rft.externalDocID=oai_openknowledge_worldbank_org_10986_2817&paramdict=en-US U7 – Book.

Blunch, N.-H. (2016). Things have changed: Returns to education in Thailand. *Journal of Southeast Asian Economies, 33*(2), 242–257.https://doi.org/10.1355/ae33-2h

References

Booth, A. (2016). Women, work and the family: Is Southeast Asia different? *Economic History of Developing Regions, 31*(1), 167. https://doi.org/10.1080/20780389.2015.1132624

Comola, M., & De Mello, L. (2011). How does decentralized minimum wage setting affect employment and informality? the case of Indonesia. *Review of Income and Wealth, 57*(1), S79–S99. https://doi.org/10.1111/j.1475-4991.2011.00451.x

David, C., & Albert, J. R. G. (2015). Primary education: Barriers to entry and bottlenecks to completion. PIDS Discussion Paper Series No. 2012–07.

Elder, S. (2014). Labour market transitions of young women and men in Asia and the Pacific, ILO Work4Youth Publication Series No. 19.

International Labor Organization. (2015). Global employment trends for youth 2015: Scaling up investments in decent jobs for youth, ILO office: International Labour Office• Geneva.

John K. (1997). The closing of the gender gap in schooling: The case of Thailand. *Comparative Education, 33*, 61–86.

Justino, P., Leone, M., & Salardi, P. (2013). Short-and long-term impact of violence on education: The case of Timor Leste. *The World Bank Economic Review, 28*(2), 320–353.

Lee, S. K., Goh, C. B., Fredriksen, B., & Tan, J. P. (2008). *Toward a better future: Education and training for economic development in Singapore since 1965*. Retrieved from http://siteresources.worldbank.org/INTAFRREGTOPEDUCATION/Resources/444659-1204656846740/4734984-1212686310562/Toward_a_better_future_Singapore.pdf

Malaysia EFA Status Report (2011). Retrieved from Korea.

McKay, A., Mussida, C., & Veruete, L. (2018). The challenge of youth employment in Asia: Lessons from four fast-growing economies. *The World Economy, 41*(4), 1045–1067. https://doi.org/10.1111/twec.12622

Mehta, A., Felipe, J., Quising, P., & Camingue, S. (2013). Where have all the educated workers gone? Services and wage inequality in three Asian economies. *Metroeconomica, 64*(3), 466–497. https://doi.org/10.1111/meca.12014

Metussin, H. (2017). Gender gap in academic achievement in Brunei Tertiary education: Qualitative perspective. *European Journal of Social Sciences Education and Research*.

Murray, T. R., Goh, K. L., & Mosbergen, R. W. (1980). Singapore. In T. Neville Postlethwaite, & R. Murray Thomas (Eds.), *Schooling in the ASEAN region*. Pergamon Press.

Oey-Gardiner, M & Sulastri (2000). Continuity, change and women in a man's world. In Oey-Gardiner, M & C. Bianpoen (Eds), *Indonesian women: The journey continues, Research School of Pacific and Asian Studies*, Canberra.

OECD. (2004). *Completing the foundation for lifelong learning: An OECD survey of upper secondary schools*. Studien Verlag Ges.m.b.H.

OECD. (2008). *The reversal of gender inequalities in higher education: An On-going trend*. Higher Education to 2030, Demography, *1*.

OECD. (2014a). *Education at a glance 2014: OECD indicators*. OECD Publishing.

OECD. (2014b). *OECD development pathways multi-dimensional review of Myanmar: Volume 2. In-depth analysis and recommendations*. OECD Development Centre.

Onphanhdala, P., & Suruga, T. (2010). Public/private school choice and internal efficiency in Lao PDR. 国民経済雑誌, *202*(4), 103–121.

Paweenawat, S. W., & Vechbanyongratana, J. (2015). Wage consequences of rapid tertiary education expansion in a developing economy: The case of Thailand. *The Developing Economies, 53*(3), 218-231. https://doi.org/10.1111/deve.12078

Pratomo, D. S. (2016). How does the minimum wage affect employment statuses of youths?: Evidence of Indonesia. *Journal of Economic Studies, 43*(2), 259–274. https://doi.org/10.1108/JES-07-2014-0131

Revilla, M., & Laarni, D. (2014). *Schooling outcomes in the Philippines, 1988–2008: Impacts of changes in household income and the implementation of the free public secondary education act (RA 6655)*.

Roberts, C. (2011). BRUNEI DARUSSALAM: Consolidating the foundations of its future? *Southeast Asian Affairs*, 35–50.

Saikia, U., Hosgelen, M., & Chalmers, J. (2011). Investigation into the population growth and its implications for primary schooling in Timor-Leste by 2020. *Asia Pacific Viewpoint, 52*(2), 194–206.

Saldanha, J., & Redden, J. (2009). Trade and youth unemployment in Timor-Leste. In *Trade and poverty reduction in the Asia-Pacific region: Case studies and lessons from low income communities*.

Skidmore, M., & Wilson, T. (2008). *Dictatorship, disorder and decline in Myanmar*. ANU E Press.

UNESCO. (2009). *National education support strategy—Philippines*. Retrieved from https://www.coursehero.com/file/12477439/uness-report/

UNESCO Institute for Statistics (UIS). (2013). Adult and Youth literacy: National, regional and global trends, 1985-2015. UIS information paper. Montreal: UIS. http://www.uis.unesco.org/Education/Documents/literacy-statistics-trends-1985-2015.pdf.

UNICEF. (2009). Gender equality in education: Education for all mid-decade assessment process.

Utomo, A. J. (2012). Women as secondary earners. *Asian Population Studies, 8*(1), 65–85. https://doi.org/10.1080/17441730.2012.646841

Open Access This chapter is licensed under the terms of the Creative Commons Attribution 4.0 International License (http://creativecommons.org/licenses/by/4.0/), which permits use, sharing, adaptation, distribution and reproduction in any medium or format, as long as you give appropriate credit to the original author(s) and the source, provide a link to the Creative Commons license and indicate if changes were made.

The images or other third party material in this chapter are included in the chapter's Creative Commons license, unless indicated otherwise in a credit line to the material. If material is not included in the chapter's Creative Commons license and your intended use is not permitted by statutory regulation or exceeds the permitted use, you will need to obtain permission directly from the copyright holder.

Chapter 7
Child Health in Southeast Asia

In the past three decades, the Southeast Asian countries have made efforts in improving child health and have seen great progress in protecting people from diseases via vaccination. It is attributable to the concerted effort by nations and global organizations, such as the WHO guidelines on nutrition for the management of severe malnutrition and overnutrition, and the National Immunization Programme (NIP) to prevent a range of diseases.

However, various socio-economic and cultural factors are intertwined in impacting the prevalence of health conditions and disease among infants and children with regional differences across countries. Of the five subregions in Asia, Southeast Asia has the second-highest prevalence and total number of children who are stunted,[1] measuring 29.4% amounting to 15.6 million, wasted,[2] measuring 9.4% amounting to 5.0 million, and underweight measuring 18.3% amounting to 9.7 million (Thet et al., 2016).

The following chapter will begin with a discussion on the prevalence of low-birthweight babies and overweight children, together with the nutrition profile of children from the severe wasting and exclusive breastfeeding rate.

7.1 Low-Birthweight Babies

According to the World Health Organization (WHO)'s definition, low-birthweight babies refer to infants whose weight at birth is less than 5.5 pounds (Hughes et al., 2017). Compared to typically developing babies, the mortality rate for low-birthweight babies is 20 times higher (McCormick, 1985; Wilcox, 2001). In 2004, the United Nations Children's Fund and World Health Organization reported that a higher number of low-birthweight babies are indicative of poorer health status

---

[1] A child's failure to attain the height expected among healthy children of same age and sex.
[2] Acute malnutrition.

in the country. Low parental education levels, young maternal age, below average mother's body measurements, and poor nutrition during pregnancy are the potential factors contributing to the high rates of low-birthweight babies (Sananpanichkul & Rujirabanjerd, 2015).

According to Fig. 7.1, most countries have 5% to 15% low-birthweight babies given each country's total number of births. A notable exception is the Philippines at 15.9%. The Philippines started at 17.9% in 1990, fluctuated over the years, and decreased to 16% in 2010. The World Bank database on Gender Statistics in 2014 marked an increase of over 22% in the last 20 years on adolescent fertility rate in the Philippines. Golding and Shenton (1990) mentioned that younger maternal age increases the probability of giving birth to low-birthweight babies.

Myanmar and Vietnam also showed a decline in low-birthweight babies over the period. Myanmar experienced a steep drop of 6% from 2000 to 2010, which can be attributed to Myanmar's increasing government health expenditure and increased access to basic health services in rural areas since 1992 (Myanmar, 2012). Vietnam showed a lesser degree of decline and dropped from 8.8% in 2000 to 5.1% in 2011. Studies showed that the implementation of a comprehensive economic reform contributed to people's consumption power for nutritious food to safeguard mothers' and babies' nutritional status. This improvement played a significant role in the decreasing trend of low-birthweight babies (Hanieh et al., 2014; Tuan et al., 2007).

However, other countries are on the opposite end of the trend with varying degrees of increase in low-birthweight babies. Thailand and Timor-Leste both experienced a sudden surge of 4–5 percentage points in one year, from 2009 to 2010 and 2002 to

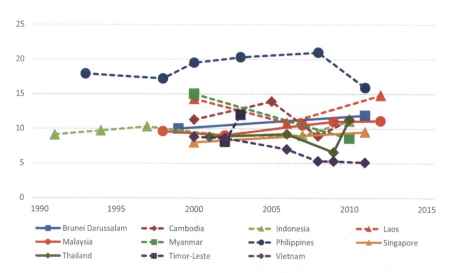

Fig. 7.1 Low-birthweight babies (% of births) of Southeast Asian countries, 1990–2015. *Source* UNICEF, State of the World's Children, Childinfo, and Demographic and Health Surveys. *Notes* Data available only for Brunei 1999–2011, Cambodia 2000–2010, Indonesia 1991–2010, Laos PDR 2000–2012, Malaysia 1998–2012, Myanmar 2000–2010, Philippines 1993–2011, Singapore 2000–2011, Thailand 2001–2010, Timor-Leste 2002–2003, and Vietnam 2000–2011

2003, respectively. Lao PDR and Cambodia experienced a drop of 3.5% to 5% before the increase to 14.8% in 2012 and 11.3% in 2010, respectively. These countries spent effort on comprehensive health care, but these schemes are yet to be comprehensive to cover all populations. For instance, in the case of Lao PDRs and Cambodia, the health coverage cannot cover all rural and provincial areas, together with the fact that there was a small formal medical workforce, the number of Cambodia and Lao PDRs inevitably increases back to a similar level in 2011 (Ministry of Health, 2013; Pridmore & Car-Hill, 2009). Events like the global food crisis in Thailand also pose challenges to Thailand's nutrition progress and hindered children and mother nutrition profile to impact on nutritional status (Heaver & Kachondam, 2002). The above situations indicated that even with governmental efforts in healthcare planning, other socio-economic factors interfere with the increasing trend of low-birthweight babies.

While there are other factors such as policy and legislation in safeguarding nutrition status, studies found that diminished policy attention on undernutrition could be due to the rising concern on overweight and obesity (Gillespie et al., 2016). The following chapter will give an overview of the trend and prevalence of overweight children, which is closely related to low birthweight rates, among Southeast Asian countries.

7.2 Prevalence of Overweight (% of Children Under 5)

WHO defines overweight for children under five years of age as weight-for-height greater than two standard deviations above WHO Child Growth Standard median. Globally, there is also a shift of trend from high-income countries to rising numbers in low- and middle-income countries, most commonly seen in urban settings (World Health Organization, 2018). Lindsay et al. (2017) found that the rapid economic growth in Southeast Asian countries has contributed to the increasing number of overweight children, particularly in urban areas. The situation is phenomenal in all countries except for Myanmar and Cambodia.

Indonesia, with the highest rate of increase, also accounted for the most number of overweight children at 11.5% in 2015. As Fig. 7.2 shows, the number of overweight children in Indonesia drastically increased from 2000 at 1.5% to 12.3% in 2010, and then it dropped slightly to 11.5% in 2013. Indonesia is followed by Thailand at 10.9% and Brunei Darussalam at 8.3% in 2009. In Thailand, it gradually rose by 9.6 percentage points (from 1.3% in 1987 to 10.9% in 2012) in 25 years. Indonesia spent only 10 years, as compared to 25 years for Thailand for the similar range of increase in overweight children. The remaining countries grew at a steady rate.

Research shows that factors such as overweight mothers before pregnancy, high birthweight of children, higher than the required portion of food taken by children, and consumption of high caloric food contribute to childhood obesity in Thailand and Indonesia (Droomers et al., 1995).

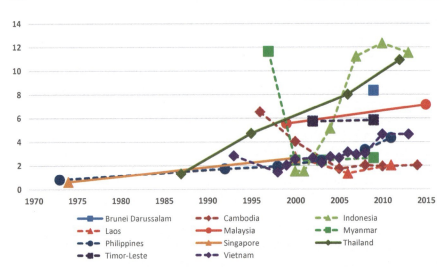

Fig. 7.2 Prevalence of overweight (% of children under 5) of Southeast Asian countires, 1974–2015. *Source* World Health Organization, Global Database on Child Growth and Malnutrition. *Notes* Data available only for: Brunei 2009, Cambodia 1996–2014, Indonesia 2000–2013, Laos PDR 2000–2011, Malaysia 1999–2015, Myanmar 1997–2009, Philippines 1973–2011, Singapore 1974–2000, Thailand 1987–2012, Timor-Leste 2002–2009, and Vietnam 1993–2014

The situation is explained by the "double burden of nutrition" (coexistence of under- and overweight) in Indonesia and "nutrition in transition" (trend from undernutrition to overnutrition) in Thailand, where urban households are the highly vulnerable ones (Mahmudiono et al., 2016; Yamborisut et al., 2006). The higher household income is contributing to improved access to high-calorie food taken by children, accompanied by low physical activities and poor parental monitoring on eating behaviour by children, creating nutritional imbalance (Yamborisut et al., 2006).

On the other end, despite a 54% increase in global childhood overweight prevalence from 1990 to 2011, both Myanmar and Cambodia show a decreasing trend. Cambodia plummeted from 6.5% to 1.7% between 1996 and 2005, while Myanmar experienced a sharp decline from 11.6% to 2.4% between 1997 and 2000 in the three years. After the fall, both countries remain at the low level at 1.7% and 2.4%, respectively. The drop in overweight children is within the same period as Myanmar's National Food Law enactment in 1997, where the law enabled people to consume quality food and initiated the prevention of harmful food habits.[3] The Ministry of Health of Cambodia also started the Health Coverage Plan in 1996 for better public access to information on health and nutrition and improving the health of pregnant mothers.[4] While the underlying reason behind the gradual decrease remains unclear, Fig. 7.1 shows that in a similar period, Cambodia experienced an increase of low-birthweight babies, starting from 2000 until 2005.

---

[3] Health in Myanmar, 2012.
[4] Cambodia Health Plan, 2008.

The above situation also created the paradox of the developing regions among Southeast Asia, where overweight, underweight, and undernutrition have coexisted due to wider socio-economic disparities. Besides Cambodia, Indonesia is one example with 11.1% of low-birthweight babies in the 2010s, and at the same time 12.3% of overweight children in the 2010s. Malaysia also faces a similar "double burden" syndrome for having more overweight counterparts than low birthweight counterparts, and not much difference for its prevalence between rural and urban areas (Mustapha, 2017). The following section will further evaluate the nutrition shift from undernutrition to overnutrition in Southeast Asian countries by looking specifically at the figure of wasting and breastfeeding rate to give a complete overview of the underlying causes and effects in recent decades.

7.3 Prevalence of Wasting (% of Children Under 5)

World Health Organization (2018) defines wasting as acute malnutrition, which refers to the sudden and drastic lack of nutrients due to sickness and lack of food availability. Wasting is a stronger predictor of mortality than stunting or being underweight (Greffeuille et al., 2016).

Most Southeast Asian countries in Fig. 7.3a are concentrated below 15% of wasting for children under 5. Timor-Leste is an exception, having the highest figure and steepest increase to 24.5% in 2007 followed by a more recent fall. About 7.5% of these children are in severe wasting (see Fig. 7.3b). Since the independence of Timor-Leste in 2002, the young nation is developing its economy and recovering from political unrest (Bank, 2011). Risk factors such as high malnutrition rate among women, early age at first birth, low contraceptive prevalence, and high fertility are all potential reasons leading to the sudden increase in wasted children (Provo et al., 2017). The upward trend is then mediated by the 2009 initiative from UNICEF and the Ministry of Health's effort in introducing the National Nutrition Strategy to all districts (UNICEF, 2013).

The prevalence of wasting is also high in Laos and Cambodia. In Lao, it was 11.8% in 1993 which subsequently reached a peak at 17.5% in 2000 and then decreased rapidly to 6.7% in 2012. In Cambodia, the rate was 13.4% in 1996 reaching a peak at 16.9% in 2000 and declined to 9.6% in 2014. In 2000, Cambodia and Lao PDR also recorded a high percentage of severe wasting at 7.5% and 7.6%, with Indonesia catching up with the trend at 6.8% in 2007 (Fig. 7.3b). Studies found that the socio-economic status of families has a strong relation to wasting. Economic inequality pertaining to mothers influence the access to nutrition for children in their first two years of age (Greffeuille et al., 2016). In the past, healthcare funding in Laos relied heavily on out-of-pocket payments. Sixty-three percentage of healthcare expenditure was sourced from household expenditure (World Health Organization, 2012). In Cambodia, health policies were influenced by political instability up till 1997, partly accounting for the peak in the percentage of wasted children in the 2000s.

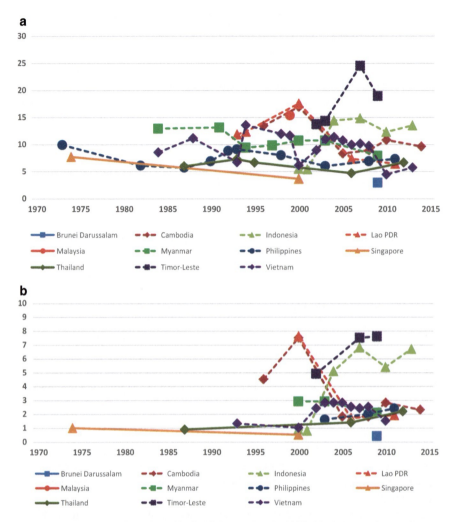

Fig. 7.3 a Prevalence of wasting (% of children under 5), 1970–2015, **b** prevalence of severe wasting, weight for height (% of children under 5), 1970–2015. *Source* World Health Organization, Global Database on Child Growth and Malnutrition. *Notes* Data available only for: Brunei 2009, Cambodia 2000–2013, Indonesia 2000–2013, Laos PDR 2000–2011, Myanmar 2000–2009, Philippines 2003–2011, Singapore 2000, Thailand 2006–2012, Timor-Leste 2002–2009, and Vietnam 1993–2010; missing data for Malaysia

Following the introduction of health policies and planning through the comprehensive Primary Health Care Policy (2000) and Sixth and Seventh National Health Sector Development Plans (2006–2010) in Laos and Health Sector Reform in Cambodia since the 1990s, these countries made impressive progress in health outcomes. There was a significant decrease in the number of wasted children starting from the 2000s (Grundy et al., 2009).

7.3 Prevalence of Wasting (% of Children Under 5)

Indonesia recorded a jump from 5.5% in 2000 to 14.4% in 2004 in the percentage measure of wasting (Fig. 7.3a). In mid-1997, Indonesia was hit by the Asian financial crisis, and purchasing power of citizens for food and health products had decreased (Bloem et al., 2000). This effect was coupled with the decentralization of the health system in 1999, which indirectly led to discrepancies in the provision of health services for the public; thus, the figure on wasting jumped rapidly starting from 2000 (Mahendradhata et al., 2017).

7.4 Exclusive Breastfeeding Rate

WHO recommends that children should be breastfed exclusively for 6 months, followed by continued breastfeeding along with the introduction of complementary (semi-solid and solid) food that is safe, appropriate, and adequate for up to 2 years of age and beyond (World Health Organization, 2018). Breastfeeding is also one of the most effective interventions in malnutrition among early childhood (Prak et al., 2014). Figure 7.4 shows that as of 2015, all countries showed an increasing trend of breastfeeding with varying degrees of increment from 2000 to 2010. The notable exception includes the decrease in Indonesia and the Philippines since early 2000.

Cambodia marks the highest percentage of breastfeeding babies peaking at 73.5% in 2010 although a decline to 65.2% in 2014 is observed. Public health campaigns

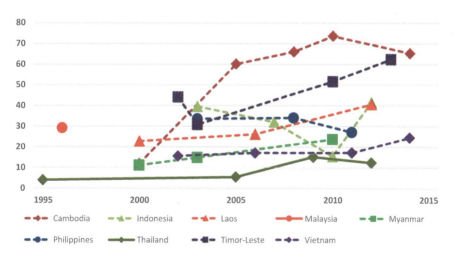

Fig. 7.4 Exclusive breastfeeding (% of children under 6 months) of Southeast Asian countries, 1995–2015. *Source* UNICEF, State of the World's Children, Childinfo, and Demographic and Health Surveys. *Notes* Data available only for: Cambodia 2000–2014, Indonesia 2003–2012, Laos PDR 2000–2012, Myanmar 2000–2010, Philippines 2003–2011, Singapore 2000, Thailand 1995–2012, Timor-Leste 2002–2013, Vietnam 2002–2014, and Malaysia 1996. Missing data for Brunei and Singapore

contributed to the high percentage of breastfeeding babies in Cambodia through effective intervention to promote and protect breastfeeding practices. But it lacked sustained effort starting in 2005 leading to a decline since 2010. A study shows that during this period, illegal promotion of breastfeeding substitutes filled the market to dislodge breastfeeding practices among vulnerable groups (Prak et al., 2014).

Timor-Leste showed a steep increase since early 2000 from 30.7% in 2003 to 62.3% in 2013. This may be attributed to the fact that maternal and child health interventions following the 5-year (2002–2006) National Development Plan (NDP) became more stable after the conflict in 2003 (Khanal et al., 2014; Thet et al., 2016; Tilman, 2004).

Myanmar marked 11% in 2000 to 51.2% in 2016. This increase can be attributed to the effort by WHO and UNICEF, which is promoting more trained workers and community support.

In contrast, Thailand and Vietnam maintain a low prevalence and a sluggish increase in exclusive breastfeeding rates for children under 6 months. Thailand is at 12.3% in 2012, and Vietnam is at 24.3% in 2014, which is lower than the world average of 35%. A review on Thailand's and Vietnam's health policy during the period of 2001 to 2016 shows that various factors facing the health professional and healthcare system, and family and social context are creating an intertwined influence on the exclusive breastfeeding rate in both Thailand and Vietnam, coupled with the premature introduction of complementary food in Vietnam (Duong et al., 2004; Thepha et al., 2017).

References

Bank, W. (2011). *Reproductive health at a glance—Timor-Leste*. Retrieved from Washington, DC: http://siteresources.worldbank.org/INTPRH/Resources/376374-1282255445143/TimorLeste52411web.pdf

Bloem, M. W., Kosen, S., Muhilal, M., Pee, S. D., Sari, M., Soekarjo, D. D., Satoto, T., Tjiong, R. (2000). Indonesia's crisis causes considerable weight loss among mothers and adolescents. *Malaysian Journal of Nutrition, 6*(2), 203–214.

Droomers, M., Gross, R., Schultink, W., & Sastroamidjojo, S. (1995). High socioeconomic class preschool children from Jakarta, Indonesia are taller and heavier than NCHS reference population. *European Journal of Clinical Nutrition, 49*(10), 740–744.

Duong, D. V., Binns, C. W., & Lee, A. H. (2004). Breast-feeding initiation and exclusive breast-feeding in rural Vietnam. *Public Health Nutrition, 7*(6), 795–799. https://doi.org/10.1079/PHN2004609

Gillespie, S., Tontisirin, K., & Zseleczky, L. (2016). Local to national: Thailand's integrated nutrition program. In *Nourishing millions: Stories of change in nutrition* (Ch. 10, pp. 91–98). International Food Policy Research Institute (IFPRI). https://doi.org/10.2499/9780896295889_10

Golding, J., & Shenton, T. (1990). Low birth-weight and pre-term delivery in South-East Asia. The WHO international collaborative study of hypertensive disorders of pregnancy. *Social Science and Medicine, 30*(4), 497–502. https://doi.org/10.1016/0277-9536(90)90352-S

Greffeuille, V., Sophonneary, P., Laillou, A., Gauthier, L., Hong, R., Hong, R., Poirot, E., Dijkhuizen, M., Wieringa, F., Berger, J. (2016). Persistent inequalities in child undernutrition in Cambodia from 2000 until today. *Nutrients, 8*(5), 297. https://doi.org/10.3390/nu8050297

References

Grundy, J., Khut, Q. Y., Oum, S., Annear, P., & Ky, V. (2009). Health system strengthening in Cambodia—A case study of health policy response to social transition. *Health Policy, 92*(2), 107–115. https://doi.org/10.1016/j.healthpol.2009.05.001

Hanieh, S., Ha, T. T., Simpson, J. A., Thuy, T. T., Khuong, N. C., Thoang, D. D., Tran, T. D., Tuan, T., Fisher, J., Biggs, B.-A. (2014). Postnatal growth outcomes and influence of maternal gestational weight gain: a prospective cohort study in rural Vietnam. *BMC Pregnancy and Childbirth, 14*, 339. https://doi.org/10.1186/1471-2393-14-339

Heaver, R., & Kachondam, Y. (2002). Thailand's national nutrition program lessons in management and capacity development.

Hughes, M. M., Black, R. E., & Katz, J. (2017). 2500-g low birth weight cutoff: History and implications for future research and policy. *Maternal and Child Health Journal, 21*(2), 283–289. https://doi.org/10.1007/s10995-016-2131-9

Khanal, V., da Cruz, J. L. N. B., Karkee, R., & Lee, A. H. (2014). Factors associated with exclusive breastfeeding in Timor-Leste: Findings from demographic and health survey 2009–2010. *Nutrients, 6*(4), 1691–1700. https://doi.org/10.3390/nu6041691

Lindsay, A. C., Sitthisongkram, S., Greaney, M. L., Wallington, S. F., & Ruengdej, P. (2017). Non-responsive feeding practices, unhealthy eating behaviors, and risk of child overweight and obesity in Southeast Asia: A systematic review. *International Journal of Environmental Research and Public Health, 14*(4), 436. https://doi.org/10.3390/ijerph14040436

Mahendradhata, Y., Trisnantoro, L., Listyadewi, S., Soewondo, P., Marthias, T., Harimurti, P., & Prawira, J. (2017). The Republic of Indonesia health system review. In *Health systems in transition*. World Health Organization.

Mahmudiono, T., Nindya, T. S., Andrias, D. R., Megatsari, H., & Rosenkranz, R. R. (2016). The effectiveness of nutrition education for overweight/obese mothers with stunted children (NEO-MOM) in reducing the double burden of malnutrition in Indonesia: Study protocol for a randomized controlled trial. *BMC Public Health, 16*, 486. https://doi.org/10.1186/s12889-016-3155-1

McCormick, M. C. (1985). The contribution of low birth weight to infant mortality and childhood morbidity. *The New England Journal of Medicine, 312*(2), 82–90. https://doi.org/10.1056/NEJM198501103120204

Ministry of Health (Feb, 2013). National plan of action for food and nutrition (2011-2015). Retrieved from https://extranet.who.int/nutrition/gina/sites/default/files/MMR%202011%20National%20Plan%20of%20Action%20for%20Nutrition.pdf.

Mustapha, K. (2017). Double burden. *New Straits Times*. Retrieved from https://www.nst.com.my/lifestyle/heal/2017/06/250675/double-burden

Myanmar, H. I. (2012). Myanmar health care system.

Prak, S., Dahl, M. I., Oeurn, S., Conkle, J., Wise, A., & Laillou, A. (2014). Breastfeeding trends in Cambodia, and the increased use of breast-milk substitute-why is it a danger? *Nutrients, 6*(7), 2920–2930. https://doi.org/10.3390/nu6072920

Pridmore, P., & Carr-Hill, R. (2009). Addressing the underlying and basic causes of child undernutrition in developing countries: What works and why?

Provo, A., Atwood, S., Sullivan, E. B., & Mbuya, N. (2017). *Malnutrition in Timor-Leste: A review of the burden, drivers, and potential response*. Retrieved from http://nus.summon.serialssolutions.com/2.0.0/link/0/eLvHCXMwrV1LTwIxEJ7wOOhNo8Z35gewWraw23ozCjFRIonogUtTd1tDJF1S4P_bKYEgZ859P-fL9Os3ADy9Y8nOnVAQECilZtoKmXVEZk3YWbwMxoqVBbMx-lv6Mea9Vz6uwTpc4Y7aQJtJkd2nwah26tBs5zknEt_Xe4CHB1Fg9Fu73y3z0D-C5lDPjD-GmnEn8DnQU7cWuceJQ5oPn7yRZxEf8BFX_nisLAb0hauPBC189pEi0cLQExxWC6Lx6GnIHEms5hRG_d7o6SXZdEFR5KuNT4yc__MJPZkr0nL-l6a2yvgfFQeo4gD5GTRc5cw5IJddbQLsEDagBZFb3ZVZSQdHkrJOoS9gsNemL_dc3xUcpmQMI9_lGhoLvzQ3UHfL-W1cvT9oZbCj

Sananpanichkul, P., & Rujirabanjerd, S. (2015). Association between maternal body mass index and weight gain with low birth weight in Eastern Thailand. *The Southeast Asian Journal of Tropical Medicine and Public Health, 46*(6), 1085.

Thepha, T., Marais, D., Bell, J., & Muangpin, S. (2017). Facilitators and barriers to exclusive breastfeeding in Thailand: A narrative review. *Journal of Community and Public Health Nursing, 03*(01). https://doi.org/10.4172/2471-9846.1000160

Thet, M. M., Richards, L.-M., Sudhinaraset, M., Paw, N. E. T., & Diamond-Smith, N. (2016). Assessing rates of inadequate feeding practices among children 12–24 months: Results from a cross-sectional survey in Myanmar. *Maternal and Child Health Journal, 20*(8), 1688–1695.https://doi.org/10.1007/s10995-016-1968-2

Tilman, C. (2004). Maternal and child nutrition in Timor Leste. *Malaysian Journal of Nutrition, 10*(2), 125–130.

Tuan, N. T., Tuong, P. D., & Popkin, B. M. (2007). Body mass index (BMI) dynamics in Vietnam. *European Journal of Clinical Nutrition, 62*(1), 78–86.

UNICEF (2013). Health, nutrition and wash. Retrieved from https://www.unicef.org/timorleste/Health_and_Nutrition_FINAL_web.pdf.

World Health Organization (WHO). (2012). Health service delivery profile: Lao PDR. Geneva, Switzerland: World Health Organization. Retrieved from http://www.wpro.who.int/health_services/service_delivery_profile_laopdr.pdf.

World Health Organization (2018). Obesity and overweight. Retrieved from http://www.who.int/news-room/fact-sheets/detail/obesity-and-overweight.

Wilcox, A. J. (2001). On the importance—and the unimportance—of birthweight. *International Journal of Epidemiology, 30*(6), 1233–1241.

Yamborisut, U., Kosulwat, V., Chittchang, U., Wimonpeerapattana, W., & Suthutvoravut, U. (2006). Factors associated with dual form of malnutrition in school children in Nakhon Pathom and Bangkok. *Journal of the Medical Association of Thailand, 89*(7), 1012–1023.

Open Access This chapter is licensed under the terms of the Creative Commons Attribution 4.0 International License (http://creativecommons.org/licenses/by/4.0/), which permits use, sharing, adaptation, distribution and reproduction in any medium or format, as long as you give appropriate credit to the original author(s) and the source, provide a link to the Creative Commons license and indicate if changes were made.

The images or other third party material in this chapter are included in the chapter's Creative Commons license, unless indicated otherwise in a credit line to the material. If material is not included in the chapter's Creative Commons license and your intended use is not permitted by statutory regulation or exceeds the permitted use, you will need to obtain permission directly from the copyright holder.

Chapter 8
Conclusion

This book shows that the patterns in family, socioeconomic and demographic changes in Southeast are complex and heterogeneous. The size of the population ranges from one of the largest countries in the world—Indonesia that has about 260 million—to one of the smallest countries in the world—Brunei that has less than half a million people. Most countries have experienced growth that has doubled or tripled their population since 1960. There have been impressive though uneven gains in the economic development in this region—ranging from countries among the world's richest and most educated such as Singapore to the world's poorest—Timor-Leste, Laos PDR, and Cambodia. Countries such as Cambodia, Lao PDR, Myanmar, the Philippines and Timor-Leste still have very low GDP per capita and high poverty rates. Gains in education and health have been similarly remarkable but varied with Myanmar, Cambodia, and Lao PDR still have less than 60% of children enrolled in secondary schools. Indonesia, Thailand, Vietnam and Cambodia have less than 30% of those aged 25 and above completed at least upper secondary education. Gender inequality in education has decreased with half of the countries having more females than males enrolled in tertiary education. In general, the level of socio-economic development and demographic transition in Southeast Asia fall between East Asia and South Asia.

Age at marriage has become later for all countries, but the range is wide; for females, it ranges from close to 30 in Singapore to early 20s in Laos PDR, Cambodia and Indonesia. While marriage remains near-universal in some countries (e.g. Laos PDR and Vietnam), we also see a substantial and growing segment of the population remains single in some countries—for example, more than a quarter of females aged 30–34 remain single in Myanmar and Singapore. In countries like Thailand and the Philippines, there is a substantial proportion of women in consensual unions.

Fertility rates have declined rapidly in all countries. Currently, about half of the countries have above-replacement fertility with Timor-Leste having the highest level (5.1 in 2014) and the other half have below-replacement fertility with Singapore having the lowest fertility level (1.2 in 2014). As a result, the overall TFR in Southeast Asia is at about the replacement level of 2.1. Adolescent fertility rates in general has been declining except for Vietnam and the Philippines. Fertility transition is still in progress with wide variations in the factors that shape this process over time and across countries. We also see a substantial proportion of women remain childless in Singapore and Thailand.

Due to the lengthened life expectancy and decline in fertility, countries in this region are growing older. Singapore in particular will enter the "super-aged population" stage (over 20% of the population aged 65 and above) within a decade, seeing a rapid increase of those 80 and above who will demand significantly greater health care needs. Fortunately, Singapore has better financial resources and human capital to address such challenges than other countries in this region. Thailand and Vietnam will also face the challenges of an aging population but have less adequate resources to handle these challenges. For these three countries, the speed of population aging is very fast, taking about 20 years or less to transition from an aging society (where 7% of the total population is aged 65 and above) to an aged society (where 14 of the total population aged 65 and above). However, other than Singapore, Thailand, and Vietnam, most countries are still relatively young now in this region. Nevertheless, because of the rapid decline in fertility in the past few decades, the speed of population ageing in the next few decades in this region will be much faster than that experienced in Western countries. These countries, however, need to improve the education attainment and human development in the population. Although education, particularly, women's education, has increased significantly, some countries still have more than half of the youth population not enrolled in secondary schools (e.g., Myanmar and Cambodia). Most countries have female employment rates higher than 50% in 2015 except Malaysia and Timor Leste.

As predicted by family sociologist William Goode (1963), family sizes have become smaller in this region. However, it is important to note that nuclear families were prevalent long before industrialization in many Southeast Asian countries. Furthermore, a majority of older adults in this region still live with or near their children. Extended families remain prevalent (e.g. 40% in Thailand in 2000) and have increased in some countries (e.g. Vietnam, Indonesia, Thailand, and Cambodia) in recent years. Alternative family forms have started to emerge such as single-parent families, step families, and on-person households. These patterns indicate that the Euro-centric assumption of the extended family as a starting point of global family change and that all family forms will eventually converge to nuclear family is incorrect.

The influence of structural and ideological changes caused by modernization and globalization on family and demographic changes is evident. However, there are changes that cannot be explained by modernization such as the high singleness rate in Myanmar despite a relatively low development and the low cohabitation rate in Brunei and Singapore despite the high development level, and high cohabitation rates in Thailand and the Philippines. The diverse culture by ethnicity and religion, kinship system, and policies in different countries (discussed in greater detail in other studies) also account for the heterogeneity seen in Southeast Asia.

Signs of the "second demographic transition" remain limited thus far in this region as cohabitation is not common (except in Thailand and the Philippines), divorce rate is relatively low in even high-income countries such as Brunei and Singapore, and out-of-wedlock births are rare even in one of the world's most modern countries—Singapore—although the total fertility rates have dipped below the replacement level since 1975 and are currently among the lowest in the world. It should be noted that fertility rates fell in a context where the majority of the population in Singapore were religious. (According to the 2015 Singapore General Household Survey, 81.5% of Singaporeans have a religion.) This is at odds with the argument that secularization as a result of a decline in religiosity leads to postmodern family behavior such as below replacement fertility and non-marital childbearing. In the case of Singapore, such trends are strongly influenced by state policies that aim at upholding the practices of "parenthood within legal wedlock" and the two-parent family type. The ultra-low fertility and high proportion of never-married and childless women in Singapore reflect a combination of the high living cost, rising aspirations for self-development, changing attitudes about marriage and parenthood, and the slow institutional adaptation to the rapid changes in women's status in the last few decades, which has made family–work life balance difficult for many young people to achieve. Singapore's experience illustrates the powerful influence of social policies in consciously striving to avoid Western family values and behaviour. In other countries, family planning policies and health and welfare policies also play important roles in explaining the family and population changes in those countries.

There are some areas for concern for children and youth including the high youth unemployment rates in countries such as Indonesia, the Philippines, and Timor-Leste, especially for young women. The unfavourable conditions in the labour market will affect young people's demographic behaviour such as marriage and parenthood. Some Southeast Asian countries such as the Philippines and Laos PDR have relatively high prevalence of low-birthweight babies. Timor-Leste, Cambodia, Laos, and Indonesia have a high prevalence of child wasting. Paradoxically, Indonesia also has the highest overweight rates for children under 5, along with Thailand. These health issues in early childhood have significant negative long-term implications for an individual's life chances and the human development of the countries.

Family changes in Southeast Asia reveal some limitations in major theoretical frameworks of global family changes that are based largely on Western experiences and assume unilinear evolution. More attention is needed in these frameworks to the unique kinship system, religion and culture norms, and the influence of public policies that also played very important roles in explaining the family diversity in this region. Rapid socioeconomic changes in this region are expected to happen in the next few decades. The family demographic and cultural contexts will shape the future development in Southeast Asia. As the economic and geopolitical influence of this region increases over time, understanding the historical trends and patterns will help one to anticipate future opportunities and challenges in development in this region.

Reference

Goode, W. J. (1963). *World revolution and family patterns*. Free Press.

Open Access This chapter is licensed under the terms of the Creative Commons Attribution 4.0 International License (http://creativecommons.org/licenses/by/4.0/), which permits use, sharing, adaptation, distribution and reproduction in any medium or format, as long as you give appropriate credit to the original author(s) and the source, provide a link to the Creative Commons license and indicate if changes were made.

The images or other third party material in this chapter are included in the chapter's Creative Commons license, unless indicated otherwise in a credit line to the material. If material is not included in the chapter's Creative Commons license and your intended use is not permitted by statutory regulation or exceeds the permitted use, you will need to obtain permission directly from the copyright holder.

Printed by Printforce, the Netherlands